SPIRITUAL PLACES

In and Around
NEW YORK CITY

EMILY SQUIRES & LEN BELZER

PARAVIEW PRESS

NEW YORK

SPIRITUAL PLACES IN AND AROUND NEW YORK CITY

Book and Cover design by Smythtype
Back cover photographs by Steve Kahn

ISBN: 1-931044-03-1

Library of Congress Catalog Card Number: 00-109348

PRINTED IN THE UNITED STATES OF AMERICA

TABLE OF CONTENTS

INTRODUCTION

*N*ew York has more to offer than any other city in the world. But we pay a price for being here: Our nerves jangle and our hearts close under the assault of noise, crowds, traffic, pollution, and the frenetic pace. We need the places on and near this island that replenish our spirit.

We enter a spiritual place for renewal, a change in consciousness, a movement from separation to connection, from stress to peace, from fear to love. Such a place quiets the mind, opens the heart, and brings us closer to our true nature.

Spiritual places come in all forms: a church or temple where people worship according to their beliefs; a gallery or museum where masterpieces speak to the human condition; institutions that teach metaphysics and methods for conscious evolution; contemplative retreats; and natural settings—those gardens, rivers, and expansive views that reach us through their beauty and call to peace. Ultimately, what we are all looking for resides within us.

Spiritual places abound in such array in and around New York City that it would be impossible to include them all under one cover. Here we have chosen to recommend the places that are special to us. May this book help the seeker find that inner place where life becomes freedom and joy.

HOW TO GET THERE

• Most places located in Manhattan are easily accessible by subway, bus or cab.

• The Metropolitan Transit Authority (MTA) customer service department will help you with any questions you might have about subway and bus transportation:
MTA Information: (718) 330-3322
Hours: Mon-Fri, 9 a.m. to 5 p.m.

• Subway maps are available at no charge from token clerks at each subway station.

• Travel directions for all places outside Manhattan are provided in the book at the end of each entry.

ICON GUIDE

 CHURCHES, TEMPLES, AND MONASTERIES

COMMUNITIES

DAY TRIPS

GARDENS

LEARNING & HEALING CENTERS

LIBRARIES AND BOOKSTORES

MUSEUMS

NATURE WALKS

OVERNIGHTS

RESTAURANTS

If a sense of the sacred is going to survive, it will have to make it in New York.

ROGER HOUSDEN, *SACRED JOURNEYS IN A MODERN WORLD*

ABBY ALDRICH ROCKEFELLER SCULPTURE GARDEN

at THE MUSEUM OF MODERN ART

11 West 53rd Street, New York, NY 10019

Tel: (212) 708-9696

Hours: Sat–Tues, and Thur: 10:30 a.m.–6:00 p.m.;
Fri: 10:30 a.m.–8:30 p.m.; closed Wednesdays.
Admission: $9.50. Students and seniors $6.50.
Members free.

Most people who go to MoMA don't come to sit in the sculpture garden and we are no exception. There's just too much to see. This was the first museum to devote its collection entirely to the modern movement and has been one of its driving forces ever since it opened in 1929.

Even for the purposes of this book, what could be more perfect than the works of Matisse, Gauguin, Van Gogh, Degas, or the Water Lilies of Monet? Of course, these just scratch

> *Every genuine work of art has as much reason for being as the earth and sun.*
>
> — RALPH WALDO EMERSON,
> *SOCIETY AND SOLITUDE*

the surface of the broad collection and exhibits that make up this pioneering institution. So go, make the rounds, keeping in mind our suggestion to choose one or two areas rather than trying to "do" the whole museum in one dizzying visit. All we ask is that you remember to save time for a long respite in the sculpture garden.

This garden is remarkably integrated with the city that surrounds it. For example, the walls that separate it from 54th street are not solid. Rather, several open spaces allow the city to blend in with the garden but never overtake it. Skyscrapers rise around it but don't intrude on the space. How can this be? We believe the reason the city and this garden go so well together is that what is inside is every bit as compelling as what is outside. The garden can easily hold its own, and offers real peace for the weary.

Opulent sculptures by such modern masters as Lachaise, Matisse, Rodin, and Picasso share the granite space with equally graceful trees, plantings, fountains, and reflecting pools in a setting both lush and open.

Sitting under a shade tree, its branches weeping into a pool, we are struck by the positive power of human creativity as it blends seamlessly with its natural counterpart. Such integration is a testament to how we humans have learned to do more than exist in the jarring hugeness of the city we have created. We belong here.

AUDUBON CENTER IN GREENWICH

613 Riversville Road, Greenwich CT 06831

AUDUBON FAIRCHILD GARDEN

North Porchuck Road, Greenwich, CT 06831

Tel: (203) 869-5272

This we know: The Earth does not belong to us. We belong to the Earth. — Chief Noah Sealth

Thest words, which appear on a bench by Mead Lake, reflect the gentle setting that surrounds it. No houses, wires, or electric buzz mar the natural sounds and sights of this sanctuary. That's what makes it a perfect spot for soul-searching as well as bird-watching.

The trails are comfortable but natural. Minimal work has been done to dam the lake. Birds, ducks, and other animals have free reign. We humans are the visitors here. In Fairchild Garden a quarter of a mile away, you will want to stay forever at Shadow Pond listening to the birds and watching the breeze ripple across the water.

In the course of writing this book, we have come to realize that most of us spiritually-oriented city-dwellers yearn for natural surroundings. The 522 acres of the National Audubon Society's center in Greenwich is such a Mecca.

We have also learned a new respect for the people who have chosen to create and tend such oases: They recognize the human need to commune with Nature. They find such spots and preserve them for just this purpose. They know that to do less to such a place is to do more. They understand how to present an "Ecostery," as environmentalist Kirkpatrick Sale calls it, and then step aside and let visitors find their way within it. We consider such work a spiritual calling.

DRIVING DIRECTIONS: Take the FDR Drive to the Triboro Bridge to Hutchinson River Parkway; or West Side Highway to the Saw Mill Parkway to the Cross County to Hutchinson River Parkway, which becomes the Merritt Parkway. Take Exit 28, Round Hill Road in Connecticut (not the first Exit 28 in New York). Turn left, go 1.4 miles to John Street; then left again 1.5 miles to a four-way stop. The refuge entrance is on the right corner. It's about 30 miles from the city, about a 40 minute drive.

AYURVEDA CAFÉ

706 Amsterdam Avenue, New York, NY 10025

(between 94th and 95th Streets)

Tel: (212) 932-2400

Hours: Lunch and dinner daily, 11:30 a.m.–11:30 p.m.

*W*hen we think of Ayurveda, we think of a mystical Indian tradition having to do with essential oils and herbs; of warm unguents drizzled on fretful foreheads by gentle women with red dots marking their third eye; of Deepak Chopra and his quantum store of knowledge which seems to embrace everything in the universe. Rarely do we think of cuisine in conjunction with this tradition, though food is at the very heart of it. Perhaps this is because there are few places in our city where you can find food cooked explicitly with Ayurveda in mind.

> *Release that which is going out. Embrace that which is coming in. Leave alone that which has not yet come. Want nothing, and embrace everything.*
>
> —FROM A BOX OF QUOTES FOR PATRONS AT AYURVEDA CAFE

One such place is the Ayurveda Café, a simple, vegetarian spot on the Upper West Side. Meals here follow the requirements for Ayurvedic balance: sattvic (pure) food that incorporates the six tastes of sweet, sour, salty, bitter, astringent, and pungent. We suggest you start with a mango lassi, a drink made of fresh yogurt and mango juice. A preset meal comes with six separate little bowls containing an appetizer, small salad, two vegetable entrees, raita, and lentils. A mound of basmati rice, a delicious fresh-made bread, and a light desert round out the meal. The price, without the lassi, is $6.95 for lunch and $10.95 for dinner.

Ayurveda is a 5000-year-old tradition of holistic well-being that comes to us from India. The word ayur means "of life," and veda means "knowledge." Ayurveda includes healing, rejuvenation, and self-realization, and is achieved through balanced foods, herbs, yoga, massage, aroma therapy, and meditation. It's a lifelong practice, and if it has lasted this long, it must work!

BOSCOBEL

1601 Route 9D, Garrison, NY 10524

Tel: (845) 265-3638

Hours: Open everyday except Tuesday,
Apr–Oct: 9:30 a.m.–5 p.m.; Nov-Dec: 9:30 a.m.–4 p.m.;
Jan–Mar: closed.
Admission: $8 for tour of house, $5 to walk the grounds.

*D*oes the redolence of lilac transport you back to springs past? Does the hum of a distant lawn mower, or the smell of fresh-cut grass remind you of barefoot summer days? Can such moments that connect us with ourselves, our past, and the particularities of nature be considered spiritual? What else, we wonder, could they be?

"Boscobel"—even the name evokes images of its opulent interiors, trimmed hedges, sweeping vistas. It began in 1804 as the dream home of States Morris Dyckman and his wife, Elizabeth. After facing many near-demolitions, the home was finally moved to its present location. A fine

> *People say that what we're all seeking is a meaning for life. I don't think that's what we are seeking. I think that what we're seeking is an experience of being alive.*
>
> — Joseph Campbell

example of Neoclassical architecture, Boscobel now overlooks the Hudson Highlands, and exceeds all expectations with its close attention to every interior detail of the Federal Period and its equally immaculate gardens.

Enter the grounds and you are drawn along a path of perfectly pruned apple trees, through a circular rose garden, and directly out to an expansive view of the Hudson with the house reigning majestically above it.

On any warm day, especially in the Spring when the blossoms are at their peak, take the time to sit beneath a topiaried canopy in the herb garden. Listen as a heady drone drowns out all other sound. This is as close as we've come to that glade Yeats talks about:

Nine bean-rows will I have there,

a hive for the honeybee

And live alone in the bee-loud glade.

For the more active, a woodland trail winds through 25 acres along the Hudson, bringing its own moments of clarity and peace.

DRIVING DIRECTIONS: George Washington Bridge to Palisades Parkway North to Bear Mountain Bridge. Cross bridge and turn left onto 9D. Go eight miles north on 9D. Boscobel is clearly marked on the left. Total: 50 miles.

TRAVEL NOTE: Several mansions like Boscobel line the Hudson. Look for Hyde Park, and Lyndhurst, or Wave Hill, for example. Yes, these places are historic landmarks, but we also think of them as oases of grace that allow us quiet moments to breathe and re-connect with ourselves.

BROOKLYN BOTANIC GARDEN

900 Washington Avenue, Brooklyn, NY 11225-1099

Tel: (718) 623-7200

Hours: Apr–Sept: Tues–Fri, 8 a.m.–6 p.m.;
weekends, holidays, 10 a.m.–6 p.m.
Oct–Mar: Tues-Fri, 8 a.m.–4:30 p.m.;
weekends, holidays 10 a.m.–4:30 p.m.

alk with us through this microcosm of world horticulture and one of the most heavenly places in all of New York. We begin with the perfect miniaturized landscape of the Japanese Hill-and-Pond Garden. Graceful trees, bushes, and flowers blush in spring, and blend lacey salmons with reds and rusts in the fall. Huge, ancient cherry trees hang into a tranquil pond, occasionally disturbed by the thrashing of neon-orange and gold carp or a gaggle of geese landing nearby.

> *To observe nature in any detail is to be spellbound by the infinite creativity and divine intelligence inherent in the cosmos.*
>
> — ALEX GREY, *THE MISSION OF ART*

Wandering among the topiaried maples and evergreens surrounding a small waterfall, we are struck once again by the innate Japanese juxtaposition of shapes, sizes, textures and colors—hard-soft, rough-smooth, large-small, and endless shades of greens, golds, oranges, pinks, and reds—with the sense of drama that allows one giant bald Cypress to preside over all. And that's just one of many spots in this splendid garden.

Lush wetness and deep, rich smells envelop us in the Steinhardt Conservatory's Tropical Pavilion. Here giant breadfruits and exotic coffee and tea plants coexist with still, mysterious palms, the whole suffused with a constant undercurrent of rushing water. The moderate climate of the Helen Mattin Warm Temperate Pavilion exudes its sweet scents of mimosa, honeysuckle, camelia, and oleander. The Desert Pavilion presents a happy jumble of aloe, euphorbia, and cochineal surrounding one giant thread palm that drips with fruit and reaches to the pinnacle of the glass house, its spent leaves hanging from it like a grass skirt.

Outside again, the Cherry Esplanade's double rows of trees stand hung in ethereal springtime bloom as children tumble on the center green. We pass Daffodil Hill, the Shakespeare Garden, Lily Pool Terrace, and so much more.

Every inch of these 52 acres is planted to perfection and intended to move gracefully across the seasons. The benefits of membership in the garden include discounts on classes and courses that are offered year-round for adults and children, free admissions, sunset picnics, discounts on gift shop items, and more. Join. Go. Do. Enjoy.

TRAVEL DIRECTIONS: BY SUBWAY: Take the D or Q train, 6th Avenue Express, to Prospect Park, then the number 2 or 3 train, 7th Avenue Express, to Eastern Parkway. BY BUS: B41, 47, 48, or 71. BY CAR: call for directions.

TRAVEL NOTE: If you like the Brooklyn Botanic Garden, you will find the New York Botanical Garden in the Bronx equally stunning.

CATHEDRAL OF
SAINT JOHN THE DIVINE

Amsterdam Avenue and 112th Street, New York, NY 10027
Tel: (212) 662-2133

*W*hen you enter from the daylight of 112th Street, it takes your eyes a moment to adjust to the interior dimness. As they do, the silent vastness of this place begins to overwhelm you. The pulpit is barely visible from the entrance. Giant pillars soar 124 feet up into gargantuan Gothic arches that pull your gaze heavenward. This is the largest Gothic Cathedral in the world and its spiritual resources are as generous as its size.

Surrounded by such grandeur, the silence of the main sanctuary reminds us of the infinity and magnificence of Creation and our humble place within it. The many side bays and seven small chapels behind the main altar are more human in scale. Daily vesper services in any one of them allow more intimate repose.

> *The gifts of grace and delight are present and abundant; the time to live and love and give thanks and rest and delight is now, this moment, this day.*
>
> —WAYNE MULLER, *SABBATH*

There are so many joyful activities to partake of here. Wide-ranging programs include everything from high Episcopal Masses to celebrations of animals where camels and elephants parade down the center aisle; from folk dances and Celtic rituals to chanting by Tibetan monks. A favorite of ours is New York's Ensemble for Early Music, a group in residence at the Cathedral. Their *a cappella* motets and use of early instruments, presented in the small Saint James Chapel, transport the heart back to the deep spirituality of the Middle Ages.

The Cathedral is an eclectic, relevant, 21st Century meeting place for people of all religions. The gift shop reflects this with its rich selection of books, arts, and crafts from around the world.

On leaving the Cathedral, you'll smell new boxwood in the small side gardens and hear sounds of peacocks, birds, and children playing—a buffer to the world outside the gates.

The Cathedral is open daily, and all are welcome. Bring a wrap because it's cool inside, even in deep summer. Call for a schedule of events, or to be put on their mailing list.

CENTRAL BAPTIST CHURCH

166 West 92nd Street, New York, NY 10025
(at Amsterdam Avenue)
Tel: (212) 724-4004
Sunday Services: 9 a.m. and 12 Noon
Wednesdays: 7 p.m. Bible Study/Prayer Meeting.

*O*ne Sunday morning we walked past Central Baptist Church and heard the sound of rousing Gospel music pouring out the front door. Neither of us was dressed for church but we were so drawn by the music that we had to peak inside. There were scores of joyous people on their feet moving rhythmically and singing along with the choir. The atmosphere was so electric that we ran home to change for the service (we live nearby).

Inside the airy sanctuary, Reverend Michel Faulkner finished announcing upcoming events,

The light of God surrounds me;

The love of God enfolds me;

The power of God protects me;

The presence of God watches over me.

Wherever I am, God is.

— Anonymous prayer

and then asked all visitors to the congregation to please stand up. We did, along with several other people, expecting some polite welcoming remarks, but what happened truly surprised us. The entire multi-ethnic congregation got up and walked around to shake hands and extend a warm welcome to each of the visitors. What a loving experience! We both felt happy to be there and realized that the sign outside, "Central Baptist Church, The Friendliest Church in New York" was true to its word.

After more Gospel singing, the Pastor, a large man with a big heart, led a prayer. His sermon rang with passion and insight, and had touches of humor that made us laugh from the belly.

At one point Reverend Faulkner said that some tourists had called before the service to find out if there was Gospel music at the church and if they could come and listen. He told them that this was not a show, but if they wanted to come and worship they were more than welcome.

We have returned often to Central Baptist Church, each time being touched by its joyous, loving celebration of the divine.

CHUANG YEN MONASTERY

2020 Route 301, Carmel, NY 10512

Tel: (845) 228-9122

Hours: 9 a.m.–5 p.m., daily.

*T*urning from a rural road onto the monastery's gravel drive, you think you're entering a country woodland. Instead, you find another world, as two huge and decidedly Oriental structures begin to loom high above the trees. Impressive indeed, but this is only the beginning of a visit to Chuang Yin Monastery, which translates into English as the Land of Adornment.

The design of both the Great Buddha Hall and Kuan Yin Hall dates back over a thousand years to the Tang Dynasty. Giant stone animals guard the entrances, and a bell several times larger than Philadelphia's Liberty Bell stands sentinel in its own outdoor tower.

We remove our shoes and enter the smaller of the two halls, richly adorned with Buddhist art and statues of Kuan Yin, the legendary Bodhisatva whose face is the apotheosis of compassion. Sweeping rows of meditation pillows invite us to pause for a moment of contemplation.

The thought manifests as the word;
The word manifests as the deed;
The deed develops into habit;
And habit hardens into character.

So watch the thought and its ways with care
And let it spring from love
Born out of concern for all beings.

— BUDDHA

The Great Buddha Hall houses a staggering 37-foot-high white Buddha. This is the largest Buddha in the Western world and it is surrounded by one thousand small Buddhas. Sweeping wooden walls bend miraculously into the ceiling, leaving the visitor in such a state of wonder that reverence is the only possible response.

Outside, the Seven Jewel Lake teems with geese, fish, and turtles, and is presided over by yet another statue of Kuan Yin. The Thousand Lotus Memorial Terrace and several other buildings adorn the sweeping 125 acres.

The totality of this experience stimulates a deep curiosity not only about the monastery, but about the Buddhist Association of the United States, a dynamic community that has put its heart and soul into creating this place.

If you become interested in the study of Buddhism, you can choose from a number of programs, including those that call for long-term stays.

Long-term residence in the Land of Adornment. Sounds like Nirvana.

DRIVING DIRECTIONS: Take Henry Hudson Parkway to Saw Mill Parkway to Taconic Parkway North. Take Carmel Exit and turn right onto 301. The Monastery is approximately 1.7 miles on the left side of the road indicated by a sign. Total: 60 miles.

CHURCH OF NOTRE DAME

405 West 114th Street ,New York, NY 10025
(between Amsterdam and Morningside Dr.)
Tel: (212) 866-1500

*B*uilt in the early 1900s, this stately vine-covered church was modeled after *L'Église des Invalides* in Paris. By all exterior appearances, this is a church of straightforward design. Upon entering, however, a surprising replica of the grotto at Lourdes, where the Virgin appeared to Saint Bernadette in 1858, rises several stories behind the main altar. It feels as if the church has been built directly into the side of a mountain, although this grotto was actually built inside after the church was completed.

> *The important thing is not to think much but to love much; and so do that which best stirs you to love.*
>
> — Saint Theresa of Avila

To the parishioners, this grotto is more than a stunning attraction. You cannot help but recall the miracle that happened to that young woman so long ago. Perhaps as a result, the statuary seems more alive here than in other places and Mary appears to glow from her place in the grotto.

In the daily Catholic masses held directly before the grotto, the few stalwarts attending clearly receive great benefit from being in this holy place. The open, French, neo-classical style creates a grand space, while its relatively small size allows a gentle intimacy.

The church is situated on the quiet corner of 114th street and Morningside Drive, overlooking the steep park across the street that slides down into Harlem. The building's massive walls and double sets of doors eliminate whatever outside noise there is and creates such profound quiet that you can hear the clack of a single pair of shoes on the marble floor, the sweep of a broom, even the breath of a fellow worshipper. Stepping into such heavenly peace allows us to shed a few layers of the protective covering we New Yorkers normally carry with us.

The church is open for a half an hour before mass each day and, of course, on Sunday.

THE CLOISTERS

Northern tip of Fort Tryon Park New York, NY 10040

Tel: (212) 923-3700

Hours: Tues–Sun, 9:30 a.m.–5:15 p.m.; closed Mondays.

Suggested donation: $8, $4 students and seniors.

Underneath all the texts, all the sacred psalms and canticles, these watery varieties of sounds and silences, terrifying, mysterious, whirling and sometimes gestating and gentle must somehow be felt in the pulse, ebb, and flow of the music that sings in me. My new song must float like a feather on the breath of God. — HILDEGARD OF BINGEN

This riveting glimpse into life in the Middle Ages is an essential place on any seeker's itinerary—especially if you were a nun or monk in a past life. The art is celestial—paintings and illuminated manuscripts, intricately woven tapestries from churches and castles, a treasury of gold, silver, jewels, ivories, and enamels—each chosen specifically for the Cloisters from the vast collection of the Metropolitan Museum of Art.

But it's the feeling of the place that makes it so rare.

Madrigals and Gregorian Chants echo through high stone-arched corridors. Chairs are set in small chapels for meditation. Beatific statues of saints and Mary with baby Jesus cast their gaze upon you.

Recent interest in such figures as the 11th century's Abbess Hildegard of Bingen have stirred a new appreciation of things Medieval, and the crucial role of herbs in the Middle Ages is being reexamined. The historically accurate garden at The Cloisters gives us an idea how some of them were used. Arcane plants like Feverfew, Agrimony, Mallow, and Burdock were used by the nuns and their parishioners for cooking, weaving, painting, as well as healing.

Espalliered pear trees work their way between Gothic buttresses under warm red-tiled roofs. Covered arched walkways enclose small gardens with chirping birds, bubbling fountains, and quince trees laden with fruit. The softest of green grass calls Rumi to mind: "When the soul lies down in that grass, the world is too full to talk about."

All this high atop a hill in Fort Tryon Park with a sweeping view of the Hudson. Hie thee there!

TRAVEL DIRECTIONS:
BY SUBWAY: Take the A train, 8th Avenue Express, to 190th Street, walk north to Fort Tryon Park. The Cloisters is at the end of the park.
BY BUS: The M4 goes directly to the Cloisters-the last stop.
BY CAR: Take theHenry Hudson Parkway North to the Fort Tryon Park exit.

CONGREGATION B'NAI JESHURUN

257 West 88th Street (between Broadway and West End)
Office: 100A West 89th Street New York, NY 10024
Tel: (212) 787-7600

*G*oing to a service at B'nai Jeshurun is like attending a warm, family get-together with people who are genuinely happy to be there. The Middle-Eastern-style synagogue is filled to capacity every Friday night for Shabat, "the hour of nightfall." Children roam the aisles and chat amiably with one another. Part of the service is reserved especially for them. They are obviously the apples of not only their parent's but everyone else's eyes as well.

Often at Shabat a guitar and several other stringed instruments are played and everyone sings the entire service. You may not be familiar with what the words mean, but the service has the cadence of a sixties love-in. On our first visit, it was so alive we

What you do in response to the ocean of suffering may seem insignificant but it is very important you do it.

—Mahatma Ghandi

34

thought that people were going to get up and dance in the aisles. Then, amazingly, that's exactly what they did. The entire congregation held hands and danced the Hora around the sanctuary, some with children on their shoulders, laughing, singing, occasionally breaking into favorite steps. It felt like one giant family all mixed together in joyous celebration.

Many other programs and services take place during the week at "BJ," as it is fondly called. Staunchly dedicated to service in the community and beyond, the service, in part, reads:

> *The heavens are the heavens of the Lord.*
> *But the earth He has given to mortals*
> *so that we might make of it something heavenly.*

CONSERVATORY GARDEN

Fifth Avenue and 105th St. New York, NY 10021

Tel: (212) 360-2766

Hours: 8 a.m.–dusk. Admission: Free.

It isn't necessary to venture into the wilds to find tranquility in our fair city. Amid the free-wheeling romantic sprawl of Central Park there reside six unexpected acres of pristine, formal gardens where even Woody Allen would feel at home.

The garden opens off Fifth Avenue through regal wrought iron gates. Your gaze is immediately drawn across a wide expanse of lawn to a formal fountain backed by a wisteria-covered pergola.

> *I am two with Nature.*
>
> — WOODY ALLEN

The shaded avenues, or crabapple *allees*, bordering this elegant expanse are a bit too accessible to allow for contemplation. But walk to the smaller south garden surrounded by groomed hedges and a soft palate of manicured plantings, and we guarantee you'll find the perfect respite.

Here, shade trees provide space for inner work, but if you love gardens as much as we do, you may want to take in this one's beauty before venturing inward.

In the small pond, a bronze boy plays a flute. Beside him, a girl holds a bowl that doubles as a birdbath before its overflow trickles down her side. A simple gateway opens to the oneness of things as you watch a chickadee immerse herself again and again in the shallows then flick the water off into bright sparkles of sunlight.

On the other side of the green, the north garden exhibits its own circular serenity. A central statue of maidens frolic in a pool surrounded by 20,000 tulips in the spring and Korean Chrysanthemums in the fall. Benches are set within arches wound with climbing roses so that you can experience this beauty while feeling secluded.

It gives us renewed faith in our tribe to see a city park set aside a place of such delicate care and beauty and label it a "designated quiet zone."

EROL BEKER CHAPEL OF THE GOOD SHEPHERD

at SAINT PETER'S CHURCH

619 Lexington Avenue at 54th Street, New York, NY 10022

Tel: (212) 935-2200

Hours: 9 a.m.–10 p.m.; Chapel Masses: Mon–Fri, 12:15 p.m.

A modern church set in the heart of a city has to be prepared for the constant challenge of traffic, crowds, and attendant noise. Acoustically isolated from the street and subway noise, St. Peter's thinks of itself as "a majestic rock, a stable monument that affirms God's presence in the heart of the city." All of this to say that this church, a congregation of the Evangelical Lutheran Church in America, understands its particular mid-town mission, and performs it admirably.

> *The Lord is my shepherd,*
> *I shall not want.*
> *He maketh me to lie down in*
> *green pastures;*
> *He leadeth me beside the*
> *still waters.*
> *He restoreth my soul.*
>
> —PSALMS 23: 1-3

Housed next to St. Peter's is the Erol Beker Chapel. This

small, five-sided space is a sculptural, monotonal work in white by the eminent artist Louise Nevelson. Sculptures of highly abstract slashes of white wood hang on stark white walls.

The chapel is so unusual and otherworldly that it may take some getting used to at first. When we first stepped into the sanctuary it felt as if there were many presences watching over us in the guise of a large multi-leveled sculpture called Frieze of the Apostles. The floors, pews, and altar are bleached to a white ash. Eventually your eyes will fasten on the chapel's altar and the gold-leafed Cross of the Good Shepherd that hangs on the wall behind it.

Nevelson wanted to create a "place of purity," an inviolate space exclusively for prayer and meditation. From the well-worn floors, it appears that she has succeeded in providing a much-needed respite from midtown's business-as-usual.

FRICK COLLECTION

1 East 70th Street and Fifth Avenue New York, NY 10021
Tel: (212) 288-0700
Hours: Tues–Sat, 10 a.m.–6 p.m.; Sun, 1–6 p.m.
Closed Monday and holidays. Admission: $7
Students and Seniors: $5

*L*ate at night, Henry Clay Frick (1849-1919) often wandered through the splendid rooms of his magnificent mansion, sitting for a spell on one couch, then another, "absorbing happiness through his eyes." And well he might, since he was looking at his own collection of some of the finest European and American paintings of his day.

Art for art's sake is an
empty phrase.
Art for the sake of the true,
art for the sake of the good
and the beautiful,
That is the faith I am
searching for.

— George Sand

From the beginning, this tough Pittsburgh coke-and-steel industrialist planned to donate his home and collected works for public viewing. His wish was that they would offer peace and harmony to anyone who visited, and he saw to it that not a single image of violence marred the collection.

As we stroll from gallery to exquisite gallery, the objects d'arts, the masterpieces by Rembrandt, Goya, Turner, Whistler, and entire rooms decorated with murals by Boucher and Fragonard, elevate us to that calm place intended by Henry Frick. Paintings such as Bellini's *St. Frances in the Desert,* Constable's *Salisbury Cathedral,* or the golden hues of Turner's *Harbor of Dieppe* transport us to the goode olde days when life was simpler.

For us, viewing art in a collector's home with its original furnishings adds a personal intimacy that no museum can match. Frick's mansion is designed in a style reminiscent of 18th Century European Beaux Arts, with parquet and marble floors and velvet sofas actually meant for sitting.

After viewing this stunning collection, we catch our breath in the Garden Court decorated with azaleas, orchids, palms, and bromeliads. Natural light slides down tall double columns while water falls from a two-tiered marble fountain—a regal setting for contemplation.

Live concerts are often performed here and, at special times during the day, visitors are treated to recitals recorded on a huge organ from the Frick collection. Listening to Couperin or Vivaldi, we never want to leave.

GENERAL GRANT
NATIONAL MEMORIAL

Riverside Drive and West 122nd Street New York, NY

Tel: (212) 666-1640

*Hours: 9 a.m.–5 p.m. every day except Christmas
and New Years Day*

A s good Upper West Siders, we work at being open to other beliefs and religions, other ethnicities. It comes with the territory, and we're proud of it. So we were quite surprised at our not-so-positive reaction when a friend recommended Grant's Tomb for this book.

Let us have peace.

— ULYSSES S. GRANT'S
PRESIDENTIAL SLOGAN

As Emily grew up below the Mason-Dixon Line where some still speak of the Civil War as "the recent unpleasantness," Ulysses S. Grant is not exactly a topic for conversation around the dinner table. And neither of us had even been inside the memorial. So, without further ado, we gathered ourselves and made the pilgrimage.

We are glad to have gone. Grant's tomb is a great deal more than a mausoleum for the former U.S. President and his wife. It provides a small history lesson on an era, a pictorial biography of the man credited with winning the Civil War, ending slavery, and reuniting the nation. Here we learn that, throughout his presidency, Grant was described as modest, calm, sincere, and unpretentious. One look into his intense face, that permanent crease between his brows, indicates a caring person committed to doing anything for peace. This experience brought about an unexpected reconciliation with a part of the past that has hung around us far too long.

For those without such odd baggage, the graceful 150-foot-high rotunda echoes the cool quiet streets that surround Riverside Church and Columbia University. Outside, the wide and shady promenade lined with comfortable benches harkens back to a calmer time when sitting for an unhurried moment to contemplate your inner thoughts was not as unimaginable as it is today.

GENERAL THEOLOGICAL SEMINARY

of THE EPISCOPAL CHURCH

175 Ninth Avenue, New York, NY 10011

(between 20th and 21st Streets),

Tel: (212) 243-5150

Hours: Winter months, Mon–Fri, 12–3 p.m.;

Sat, 11 a.m.–3 p.m.; Closed Sunday. Admission: Free

*R*ilke thought academic communities connected us with "the grace of great things." Thomas Merton called the sense of community the "hidden wholeness." Such completeness radiates from the people who have come together to study at the General Theological Seminary.

The Seminary's venerable red brick buildings, erected mostly in the late 1800s, are in an English Collegiate Gothic style reminiscent of Oxford. They surround a grassy commons, or "close," with the small Chapel of the Good Shepherd sitting at its hub.

This is a working institution for prospective Episcopalian clergy. However, the grounds, with bright green grass sur-

We must be the change we wish to see.

— GHANDI

rounding small gardens and lining the walks, are open to the public, as are the library and chapel. Attending an evening vespers service gives the visitor a sense of the student body: Dressed often in jeans and sandals, these seminarians need no outer proof of what is central to their lives. What pomp there is comes out of reverence, not show. These are genuine people leading committed lives, and it is uplifting to be surrounded by them, if only for a brief time.

Take a look at the pictures of the grand old library, now torn down, and the refectory which has been called the most beautiful room in all of New York (but is, alas, off limits to visitors). On one excursion, St. Mark's Library was exhibiting highlights of works by T.S. Eliot, which sent us directly to the Seminary's bookstore for a copy of his collected poems, and these words:

> *Flesh and blood is weak and frail,*
> *Susceptible to nervous shock;*
> *While the True Church can never fail*
> *For it is based upon a rock.*

Enjoy this moment of wholeness.

GREENBROOK SANCTUARY

P.O. Box 155, Alpine, New Jersey 07620-0155

Tel: (201) 768-1360 or (201) 784-0484

Hours: Sunrise to sunset.

Admission: $30 yearly for individual membership.

*W*elcome to our best-kept secret. A scant 15 minutes from the George Washington Bridge, Greenbrook Sanctuary offers a carefully laid-out surround of trails, streams, brooks, and spectacular overlooks where you can shed the layers of city tension and reunite with All That Is.

Let us take you for a walk. As we enter the trail to the Palisades, its leafy shelter cools the summer heat immediately. The mossy trail feels soft underfoot. A brief walk over the rise reveals a rocky promontory and voila!—a view for miles up and down the Hudson River.

Let's sit a moment and watch a seagull ride the same zephyrs that rise from below, shimmer through

As the crickets' soft

autumn hum is to us

So are we to the trees

As are they to the rocks

and the hills.

— GARY SNYDER

the trees, and soothe our brows. A silver train slithers silently along the opposite river bank, perhaps reminding us of a time when things existed in simpler proportion.

Ready to explore further, we follow the small grassy path right along the edge of the Palisades, then up over blue rock and into a lacy forest. It's quiet enough here to pick up nearby rustles of small animals in the leaves or the glassy trill of a wood thrush in the distance. The path leads down the hill to Greenbrook pond where countless birds and other wild creatures nest in peace.

Walking to the far end of the pond, where the water runs off in cascades, we get a sense of the whole place— 65 acres of preserve for all things natural. It's remarkable there are so few people here, so little human disturbance. If we feel adventurous, there is a walk around the pond on barely-discernable trails with spots to rest and blend into the natural world. Eventually our walk brings us to the bog, where a bridge affords a view of the microworld of tadpoles and other miniscule beings that complete this small circle of biodiversity. What a wonder to watch Nature as She replenishes herself.

We return for a brief visit to the sanctuary's museum, a repository for findings and notations of unusual sightings. Outside, a huge wild turkey grazes beneath the multiple bird feeders that finches and doves share above. So much life in such a small, sacred space.

PLEASE NOTE: *A trip to Greenbrook requires some pre-planning as you will need to join in order to receive a key to unlock the gates to the Sanctuary.*

TRAVEL DIRECTIONS:

BY SUBWAY AND BUS: Take the A train, 8th Avenue Express, to 175th Street/George Washington Bridge Bus Terminal. Take Red and Tan Lines bus 9A. Tell bus driver to stop at Greenbrook Sanctuary in Tenafly, New Jersey. Return trip across street at 36 minutes past the hour. Round trip: $6.

BY CAR: Cross the George Washington Bridge to Palisades Pkwy. Take the Parkway to Exit 1, Englewood Cliffs, turn Right onto 9W. Go 2.6 miles and look carefully for the entrance, a drive under double arches of the Palisades overhead. It isn't marked. Driving time: About 15 minutes from the bridge.

HAMMOND MUSEUM AND JAPANESE STROLL GARDEN

Deveau Road, North Salem, NY 10560
Tel: (914) 669-5033
Hours: Wed–Sat, 12–4 p.m. April–Oct

Author and spiritual gardener Judith Handelsman says a garden provides a sense of communion that "heightens our experience of love in the world. And that is what spirituality is all about: growing in love." Traditional Japanese gardens are designed to enhance this inner growth, so whenever we hear about such a place, we make it part of our travels.

A winding drive brings us to gentle, settled Hammond Museum and Stroll Garden. An Oriental garden house opens onto a small pond presided

*Ten thousand flowers
    in Spring,
The moon in autumn,
A cool breeze in summer,
    snow in winter.
If your mind isn't clouded
    by unnecessary things,
This is the best season of
    your life.* —WU-MEN

50

over by an unseen bullfrog. As we crunch along the gravel walk, he lets loose his watery bellow, swiftly answered by the throaty chant of smaller fry. If we sit still long enough on one of the shady benches, we can watch them come out to sun themselves on the warm rocks, along with a black turtle or two.

In summer, the pond is rimmed by a thick row of deep yellow irises. Iridescent dragonflies scout the perimeter, as birds chirp and flit on the soft breeze. A small island in the middle of the pond hosts a humble stone statue that bows its head in welcome.

Along the paths, we discover more plantings, statues, or simple, well-placed stones, juxtaposed to draw us into the garden's internal harmony. In a sand area, visitors are encouraged to rake their own Zen garden.

The small gallery hosts monthly exhibits, many of which revolve around Eastern themes. "Brush With the East," an exhibit of Chinese Brush Painting, was up on our last visit. The Silk Tree Cafe serves lunch from May through October in a pretty courtyard between the museum and garden.

DRIVING DIRECTIONS: From Interstate 684 North, take Exit 7. Turn right at top of ramp. Follow Route116 East for 4 miles. At stop sign, turn left onto June Road. Go ¼ mile, then right onto Deveau Road. A one-hour drive.

HANGAWI KOREAN RESTAURANT

12 East 32nd Street, New York, NY 10016
(between Fifth and Madison Avenues)
Tel: (212) 213-0077
Hours: Open for lunch and dinner. Moderately-priced.

Can a restaurant be a spiritual place? Of course it can, especially if its owners are people like Ryoon and Terri Choi, whose native Korean mountains and villages inspire the restaurant. The interior is reminiscent of a Korean temple with traditional pillars, natural wood, stone, and copper.

Hangawi calls itself "A vegetarian shrine in another space and time." When you grasp the iron ring on its mahogany door, be prepared to enter not just a gourmet Korean vegetarian restaurant, but a sanctuary as well.

In the stone entranceway, we remove our shoes in the Asian tradition, showing respect for the house we are visiting. Seated on cushions at a low

Anytime we eat, it's holy. We should have ritual and ceremony, not just gobbling down some food just to keep alive.

—M.F.K. FISHER

52

wooden table, we rest our feet in the sunken space below, while a waiter dressed as a temple monk lights a Buddhist prayer candle. All the while, otherworldly sounds of Zen music pulse softly in the background, and we feast our eyes on hand-sewn, traditional Korean silk quilts hanging from the walls, and handmade pottery displayed on wooden shelves and in wall niches.

Thus soothed, we turn to a menu of dishes so new to our palate that all expectation must be set aside: pumpkin porridge, mung bean vermicelli, Korean pancakes, sweet lotus root with sesame, chili cabbage, and exotic tofu dishes. The selection of teas alone will suit the most adventurous palate: red ginseng, date paste, mushroom, lily root, fresh green leaf. For desert, we throw caution to the wind and opt for silky chocolate tofu pudding.

What raises the level of this space from mere restaurant to internal respite is the intention and authenticity that hold us gently in the present moment.

HIMALAYAN INSTITUTE
of NEW YORK
AT EAST/WEST BOOKS
78 Fifth Avenue and 13th Street, New York, NY 10011
Tel: (212) 243-5995

*I*f you've been looking for Yogic practices and holistic medical treatments, you will appreciate the Himalayan Institute for providing it all under one roof.

While a wide range of modern Yoga techniques are taught in the city, the Himalayan Institute prides itself on maintaining the purity of classical, time-honored postures. They offer numerous Hatha Yoga, breath work, and meditation programs, even "Yoga for Kids" five through eight, and "Gentle Yoga" for those of us with physical limitations.

Their Center for Health and Holistic Medicine is located at the large Fifth Avenue branch. Physicians here are trained in homeopathy and ayurvedic as well as western medicine. The Center provides the full range of alternative modalities including acupuncture, acupressure, biofeedback, kinesiology, massage therapy, and reflexology.

The Institute's bookstore, East-West Books, is possibly better known than the organization itself. It's the largest of its kind anywhere, and if you love books on metaphysics, psychology, consciousness, spiritual teachers, holistic health, and nutrition, here you'll feel like a kid in a candy store. Recently, we found *The Spiritual Teaching of Ramana Maharshi*, a classic Len had always wanted to read. The store also offers videos, music CD's, audio cassettes, as well as various spiritual accoutrements like incense, essential oils, jewelry, statuary, and greeting cards.

The Institute was founded by Sri Swami Rama in 1971. Since then it has established centers throughout the United States, Canada, Europe and Asia. Its goal is to help people grow physically, mentally, and spiritually by combining the best knowledge of both East and West.

The international headquarters of the Himalayan Institute rests on a 400-acre campus near the town of Honesdale in northeastern Pennsylvania, a two-and-a-half-hour trip from Manhattan. Here you can participate in weekend meditation retreats, seminars on spirituality, or month-long residential programs that provide an environment for gentle inner progress.

CALL FOR TRANSPORTATION INFORMATION.

HINDU TEMPLE SOCIETY
of NORTH AMERICA

45-57 Bowne Street Flushing, NY 11355

Tel: (718) 460-8484

*O*n a small street in Flushing Queens, there resides a *bona fide* Hindu Temple just like those you might imagine in cities and towns all over India. By many accounts, this is the heart of New York's Hindu community.

Intricate carvings of deities rise high above the entrance. Every corner of the large, comfortable sanctuary houses shrines, or sanctums, to deities. The center is reserved for the main Shrine to Lord Anesh. Statues of deities abound, each lovingly adorned with fresh flowers. A light, fruity incense informs the air. Worshippers busy themselves over a large basin, breaking coconuts to be blessed and later eaten. At least one of nine resident priests can be found ringing bells, chanting, or saying prayers and blessings for devotees.

> *When I know that I am nothing, that is wisdom. When I know that I am everything, that is love.*
>
> — NASARGADATU

The prayerful walk around the shrines murmuring their own devotions. Often the sounds of a happy wedding emerge from the auditorium below.

This place has real soul. You sense it in the generosity of the people you meet. You feel it in the familiarity the devotees have for it. Every weekend a continuous stream of three to four thousand come to worship here, which may give a cue as to the best time to visit!

Uma Mysorekar runs the temple. She is a kind, down-to-earth woman with deep understanding. Many a novice has obviously asked her to make some sense of all the various gods in the Hindu religion. She explains it to us this way: There is only one God, but this God can be perceived in many different forms, each representing a quality such as wisdom, knowledge, wealth, or strength. Each of these qualities is represented by a deity. A devotee, then, may resonate with one particular deity, or aspect, more than another, while understanding that all are part of the One. "It is a simple concept, really," she says. She also calls this temple a universal place and invites everyone to come.

TRAVEL DIRECTIONS:
BY SUBWAY: Take the number 7 train, Flushing Local, from Times Square to last stop—Main Street, Flushing.
BY BUS: Take the Q27 from Main Street to Holly Ave. Walk to Bowne Street.
BY CAR: Midtown tunnel to Long Island Expressway, then take Exit 24 at Kissen Blvd and turn left onto Kissena. Go 1 mile and turn right on Holly Avenue, then three blocks to Bowne Street.

HOSPITAL CHAPELS

Some time ago, we went to a hospital to be with a friend. After she was taken into surgery, we looked around for a quiet alcove or lounge where we could be with her in spirit. But we never found such a place. Months later, someone asked if we had looked for the hospital's chapel. The thought had never dawned on us.

Since then, we have had occasion to be in several hospitals and have taken the time to look for their chapels. To our surprise, there was a chapel in almost every one, each with its own peaceful and reassuring quality. Unlike the harsh fluorescent lighting in the rest of the hospital, here it is soft and often dimmed. There is no paging system, no staff bustling by, no feeling of emergency to distract from your meditation. Rather, they are quiet, soft, cool, often with fresh flowers and stained glass windows. They are actual chapels, with a feeling of devotion and prayer about them.

A wise man should consider that health is the greatest of human blessings and learn how by his own thoughts to derive benefit from his illnesses.

—HIPPOCRATES

There are thirteen major hospitals in Manhattan and most of them have chapels. They are either interdenominational, or have areas devoted to each of the major religions. At Mount Sinai's Guggenheim Pavilion there is even an additional chapel for the Orthodox Jewish community.

So if you're visiting someone in a hospital and have the need to be alone with your thoughts, a good place to do it is right in the hospital's own chapel.

HOUSE OF THE REDEEMER

7 East 95th Street, New York, NY 10128
(between Fifth and Madison Avenues)
Tel: (212) 289-0399

Tucked away on the Upper East Side sits a gorgeous Italian Renaissance-style Palazzo that now describes itself as "dedicated to providing peace and serenity for those who seek a place apart."

Its architecture is quite remarkable. The first floor houses a dining room large enough to seat eighty people comfortably. Across the ample entryway, a large reception room welcomes visitors in handsome old-world style. Walk up the winding staircase to the authentic 15th century Italian library and sublime chapel with its intricate ceiling and floor-to-ceiling leaded-paned windows. Above are two floors of rooms, varying from singles with baths down the hall to suites with private baths. The

Let the words of my mouth
And the meditation of my
* heart,*
Be acceptable in thy sight,
O Lord my strength and
* my redeemer.*

—Psalms 19:14

60

prices vary accordingly, but you would be hard-pressed to find a better price anywhere else in New York.

Yet don't think of this simply as a place to stay when you want to come to New York for the weekend (though it is right off Fifth Avenue and wonderfully close to the Metropolitan, the Guggenheim, and Central Park). Owned and cared for by the Episcopal Church, it serves as a refuge, a place for reflection. The House lends itself to group and individual retreats, conferences, and meetings. There is always a priest in residence for counseling and help in structuring your stay, as well as many places for quiet and meditation.

What strikes us most about the House of the Redeemer is that, with all of its splendor, it remains quite authentic, open and spare. There is little here to clutter your thoughts. On the other hand, the décor is far from institutional. The rooms are kept very much as they must have been when it was a private residence of the great granddaughter of Cornelius Vanderbilt.

This is a special place, indeed. As a result, be advised that it is much in demand and reservations must be made way in advance.

HUDSON RIVER GREENWAY TRAIL
at NYACK BEACH PARK

Tel: (845) 268-3020

Hours: 8 a.m.–5 p.m. Admission: $4

Without the oxygenating breath of the forests, without the clutch of gravity and the tumbled magic of river rapids, we have no distance from our technologies, no way of assessing their limitations, no way to keep ourselves from turning into them.

—DAVID ABRAM, THE SPELL OF THE SENSUOUS

Just half an hour from the city, a rare and unusual confluence of natural treasures awaits you. Here, a seven-mile foot-and-bicycle trail runs directly alongside the Hudson River. What makes this so spectacular is that directly on the other side of this wide cinder path the magnificent Palisades soar overhead. A walk along the Hudson River Greenway Trail connects a cityphile with some of the most potent forces of nature.

We come here to drink in the fresh air wafting from the river, to listen to its waters lapping against the huge boulders at our feet, to watch hawks riding the updrafts of the jagged cliffs, and to absorb it all as spiritual nourishment.

In the dense forest beneath the cliffs, we have spotted a myriad of wild flowers, heady honeysuckle, and jumbles of blackberries ripe for picking in August. Dotted along the way, cozy benches and picnic tables provide perfect sanctuaries to sit and gaze at the spectacle of cliff converging into river. Meditating on flat boulders with the water inches from your toes and the steep shade of the forest rising protectively at your back will bring you to a state of vibrant peacefulness and connection.

You would think such a place might be overrun with people longing to commune with the elements, but even on a Sunday in the summer it is not the least bit crowded.

The park has a carry-in, carry-out policy which means there's no place to discard containers of left-over food. So be prepared to carry out whatever your stomach can't.

DRIVING DIRECTIONS: Take the George Washington Bridge to the Palisades Parkway. Then take Exit 4 to 9W North. Follow to Nyack. Turn right onto Route 59 East to Broadway. Follow to park. Driving Time: about 30 minutes.

❖ ℕ
ISAMU NOGUCHI
GARDEN MUSEUM

32-37 Vernon Blvd (at 33rd Road)
Long Island City, Queens, New York
Tel: (718) 721-1932

Hours: Apr–Oct, Wed–Fri: 10 a.m.–5 p.m.; Sat–Sun,
11 a.m.–6 p.m. Suggested Admission: $4

O n the first floor of this indoor/outdoor gallery, monolithic pieces of rock confront you with the ancient energy of basalt and granite–rough, chiseled, raw. Isamu Noguchi referred to these stone pieces as "the bones of the earth." It's sculpture of such power that you don't just look at it, you feel it.

The garden reflects the artist's view of space as a challenge to be sculpted. Large pieces rest on chunky gravel shaded by a canopy of Birch, English Ivy, and a strong Japanese Katsura tree. Noguchi believed that environment is our sculpture, that it is to be lived and experienced. This intentional relationship between human and nature creates a profound context for contemplation.

Nature, both in whole and in many parts, is magically self-reflective and aware.

— TERENCE MCKENNA

In contrast to the massive outside sculptures, the pieces in the upstairs gallery are more refined in both material and execution. Walking higher, it feels as if we are moving up into the softer aeries of this man's genius until, finally, in the little café at the top, we come upon his delicate paper Akiri light sculptures. All this from one man.

On one visit we were both particularly stirred by a prototype of a sculpted human face that Noguchi wanted made large enough to be seen from the moon. His motivation for this project was the horror he felt over the dropping of the atomic bomb on his homeland. At least, he felt, intelligent life from other planets would know that humans once lived here.

This garden is a bit of a trek, we grant you, but it's worth it. Ask at the desk for a list of restaurants in the area and check out P.S.1 Contemporary Art Gallery, within walking distance at 22-25 Jackson Avenue at 46th Street. Of special interest, weather permitting, is James Terrell's exhibit "Meeting," the actual experience of day turning into dusk.

SUBWAY DIRECTIONS: Take the N train, Broadway local, to the Broadway stop in Queens. From Broadway and 31st walk toward New York skyline and Vernon Blvd. Take a left and walk two blocks. Please call for shuttles available from Manhattan on weekends and for directions by car.

JOHREI FELLOWSHIP

116 Lexington Ave., 2nd Floor, New York, NY 10016

(near 28th St.)

Tel: (212) 684-0009

Hours: Mon 4 p.m.–8 p.m.; Tues–Fri 12 p.m.–8 p.m.;
Sat 12 p.m.–6 p.m.; Sun 12 p.m.–4 p.m.

The underlying principle in Johrei is that through the practice of truth, virtue, and beauty in daily life, the three major sufferings of humanity—disease, conflict, and poverty—can be transformed into a state of health, peace and prosperity.

This small, friendly fellowship hall, located directly above the bustle of Spring Street, welcomes but never overpowers the visitor. Simple Sangetsu flower arrangements temper the spare Oriental feeling of

> *Excellence is a habit. You are what you repeatedly do.*
>
> —Don Donato Castelli,
> Scientist, Priest

natural wood and calligraphy on the walls. Sangetsu, one of the three practices of Johrei, attempts to bring out the hidden beauty of flowers, rather than imposing your will on their arrangement. Johrei uses this unique art form to balance human creativity with natural beauty.

Johrei healing, the second practice, provides a path of service for its trained practitioners. They perform healings on anyone who asks. You sit across from a silent man or woman who directs spiritual energy toward you through their hands. Johrei followers believe this work activates a natural purifying process which promotes inner spiritual balance and eases physical, mental, and emotional stress. The session lasts about twenty minutes or so, and there is no physical contact. You may receive Johrei as often as you wish. It is offered free of charge, though donations are accepted.

We are least familiar with Nature Farming, the third aspect of Johrei practice, although it appears to adhere to the forward-thinking goals of growing healthful, organic food in an ecologically sustainable manner.

The Johrei Fellowship was founded in 1935 by Japanese philosopher, poet, and artist Mokichi Okada. It is described as an international association of individuals from many countries, cultures and faiths, joined together in a common spiritual practice. In addition to healings, the center also offers courses on all of its practices.

METROPOLITAN MUSEUM OF ART

Fifth Avenue and 82nd Street, New York, NY 10028

Tel: (212) 535-7710

Hours: Tues–Thurs, Sun: 9:30 a.m.–5:30 p.m.;
Fri and Sat: 9:30 a.m.–9:00 p.m.
Closed Monday. Suggested donation:
$10, $5 students and seniors, children free.

t takes days to make even a dent in the vast labyrinth that is the Met, so remember you're only human. We suggest that you decide what you want to see, then stay only a reasonable amount of time. On your way, visit some of these spots for repose and internal reflection—all in an effort to avoid what William James referred to as "an aesthetic headache."

Art of any profundity can be appreciated only slowly, gradually, in leisurely contemplation.

—Daniel Gregory Mason,
Artistic Ideals

Temple of Dendur

Two small brown build-ings covered in ancient hieroglyphs and carvings are set in a giant hall. A still black pond represents the River Nile. A wall of glass offers a silent view of Central Park and Upper Fifth Avenue. Is it the immensity of the space that creates such hushed reverence? Or is it the idea that you are sitting before the same temple where Nubians once worshipped the Goddess Isis of Philae in 15th century BC?

Astor Court

The world view of Yin (dark, void, soft, yielding, wet) and Yang (bright, solid, hard, unyielding, dry) forms the basis for much Chinese thought. In this Ming Dynasty scholar's garden, as in many Chinese gardens, a Yin-Yang balance is created by the interplay of splashing water and immovable rock.

You enter through a circular passageway guarded by two stone lions. A covered walkway spans two sides of the garden, the exuberant upswing of its tiled roof answered by a small gazebo across the court. Natural light shines onto large rugged rocks, spare Chinese plantings, and a trickling waterfall, the whole creating a true sanctuary.

Take time to let the peace of this place envelope you and replenish your energies for the rest of your journey.

The Sackler Buddha Room
Chinese Art Section

Long benches sit across from a giant Buddha mural, guarded at either end by two immense statues of Buddha. The juxtaposition of ancient pieces against stark white walls lends a sense of timelessness and room enough to direct your thoughts inward to those thousand regions in your mind yet undiscovered.

Room from the Nur Ad-Din House
Islamic Art Section

The moment you step inside this room, the sounds of the museum slip away and you are surrounded by an ornate yet spare chamber. A small fountain gurgles at your feet and high stained glass windows let in filtered sunlight. Unfortunately, you can only imagine yourself meditating on one of those comfortable cushions lining the carved wooden walls. There is no place to sit here.

The Iris and B. Gerald Cantor Roof Garden
Third floor

Modern outdoor sculpture with a stunning backdrop of Central Park and the skyscrapers beyond make this the perfect place to contemplate man's considerable handiwork within an equally considerable natural context. Great when the weather is great.

Christmas at the Met
Medieval Section

If you're willing to brave the hordes of visitors around the holidays, a treat awaits you in the Medieval Section. The beautifully-decorated Christmas tree in this perfect setting provides a touching connection with the past and a reminder of the continuity of the species.

MOHONK
MOUNTAIN HOUSE

New Paltz, NY 12561
Tel: (845) 255-1000; Schedule: 1-800-722-6646
Hours: Open all year.

Walk leisurely, don't drive, walk in the garden,
don't answer the phone, turn off the television
and the radio, forget the CD and the computer.
Quiet the insidious technology, and remember
that we live in bodies that, through a feast of the
senses, appreciate the beauty of the world.

—WAYNE MULLER, *SABBATH*

When Quaker twins Albert and Alfred Smiley discovered Lake Mohonk in 1869, they immediately envisioned a peaceful retreat for people to enjoy nature, and a place to renew not only the body, but the mind and spirit as well. Ever since then, the 2200-acre National Historic Landmark has been owned and operated by the Smiley family, which has maintained and refined that original vision.

Inside, endless Victorian halls meander around wooden staircases to large wood-paneled meeting rooms, a dining room that manages to be at once vast and homey, and 275 private rooms, many with their own fireplaces.

Outside, Mohonk Mountain House is a splendid architectural jumble of stone and wood facades topped with roofs and turrets made of everything from cedar shakes to tin and tile. This maze reflects the many expansions over the decades required to accommodate a multitude of visitors who have come to think of Mohonk as their second home.

The Castle, as the house is sometimes called, presides over a pristine mountain lake that is half a mile long and sixty feet deep. Its broad porches lined with rocking chairs beckon visitors to drink in spectacular views of unspoiled nature. For those so inclined, activities abound. Children are welcome, and nature walks, arts, crafts, and games provide them with so much to do that even the smallest visitors seem continually filled with delight.

Thoreau spoke of Nature as being "full of genius, full of the divinity." For those of us who have limited access to the out-of-doors, yet yearn to be in touch with it, this is such a place. Choose a stroll through perfectly-tended gardens, or a hike along trails around the lake and up the mountain-top to gaze out onto thousands of acres of unspoiled land. Opportunities for reflecting and communing with Nature abound, and charming handmade benches and gazebos are placed strategically along the trails and in the gardens for such moments.

From its calendar of events to the care of its guests, Mohonk exudes a gentle, well-considered spirituality. To spend time in a place of such transcendent beauty among people so obviously happy to be here refreshes the spirit and makes us better able to negotiate the slings and arrows of the world below.

TRAVEL DIRECTIONS:

BY BUS: Adirondack Trailways from Port Authority Bus Terminal to New Paltz, New York. Trip is 1 hour 35 minutes. Fare: $33.95 round trip. Cab fare from bus station: around $15. If you're staying overnight, call 24 hours in advance and a courtesy car will pick you up.

BY CAR: 90 miles north of Manhattan in the Hudson Valley. From Exit 18 off the New York State Thruway(I87 North), Mohonk is 6 miles west of New Paltz.

NEW YORK BUDDHIST CHURCH/JODOSHINSHU BUDDHIST TEMPLE

331-332 Riverside Drive, New York, NY 10025
(between 105th and 106th Streets)
Tel: (212) 678-0305
Services: Sun, 11:30 a.m.
Meditations: Mon–Fri, 6:30–7:30 a.m.

How many times have you driven up Riverside Drive and wondered about that large standing bronze figure wearing a broad-brimmed hat and set back under an opaque canopy? This statue came from Hiroshima where it withstood the atomic blast before being brought here to America. The figure is Shinran Shonin (1173–1262), the founder of the Jodo Shinshu sect of Buddhism, which is practiced in its modest church/temple at 105th and Riverside Drive.

This particular form of Buddhism has developed as a practice accessible to lay people, unlike other more

Our true home is in the present moment. The miracle is not to walk on water. The miracle is to walk on the green earth in the present moment.

—THICH NHAT HANH

monastic sects. In fact, Shinran Shonin was the first practicing Buddhist monk to be officially married with a family. T. Kenjitsu Nakagaki, the young Sensei who heads this congregation is also married.

Services are conducted in both English and Japanese. Other programs are available, such as beginning meditation, programs for children, martial arts, brush painting, and taiko drumming.

The congregation also owns the beautiful townhouse next door, an historic landmark built by William Randolph Hearst. Meditation classes are held here in one of the most beautiful meditation rooms we know of in the city.

The church/temple itself is small and unprepossessing, but its altar is quite ornate and beautiful. Most importantly, the small congregation is obviously closeknit as well as being open and inclusive. Save some time for coffee or lunch afterward where you can get to know these lovely people.

When asked why this is called a church rather than a temple, we were reminded by the Sensei that, when this congregation was formed 60 years ago, there was a great deal of prejudice and pressure against minority religions, especially those from Japan. In an effort to become less visible, a great many tried to conform, to "Americanize," by calling themselves churches. Maybe now it's time to drop the "church" and call it the Jodoshinshu Buddhist Temple.

NEW YORK CHINESE SCHOLAR'S GARDEN
SNUG HARBOR CULTURAL CENTER
1000 Richmond Terrace, Staten Island, NY 10301-9926
Tel: (718) 448-2500

*S*itting beneath the rippling Meandering Cloud Wall, gazing across the still pond toward the Moon Gate of Uncommon Beauty and the Assured Tranquility Pavilion at the New York Chinese Scholar's Garden, we marvel yet again at the lengths to which humans go to create harmonic settings for the mind and spirit.

The Chinese have had centuries to perfect such settings, and this new garden, created in the style of the Ming Dynasty, is a splendid representation of that art. The precise use of wood, rocks, water, plantings, walkways, and pavilions build a textured environment of depth and expansiveness. The pathways are painstakingly laid in black stones

Hills and valleys in my mind

Looking at intricate rocks

and wispy streams

Ideas of pictures come from

the horizon.

—CALLIGRAPHY FROM
SCHOLAR'S GARDEN

set on their sides, interwoven with white stones laid flat. The juxtapositions of dark tiled roofs with stark white walls, craggy stone with soft green vegetation, and still ponds with falling water emphasize the creative tension people feel in so much of Chinese philosophy.

A place such as this is rife with meaning and intention. Rock signifies the skeleton of the earth, waterways reflect its arteries. Pine, bamboo, and plum symbolize characteristics such as aloofness, pride, and endurance. Even the furniture in a scholar's garden is referred to as its internal organs. You feel an undeniable, textural connection with All There Is in this serene harmonious space.

Prepare to spend some time here. The garden has been designed to create endless views and to evoke a sense of infinity within a limited space. You can wander this single acre and never see the same vista twice.

TRAVEL DIRECTIONS:
BY FERRY AND BUS: Take the Ferry to Staten Island.
Take #S40 Bus at Ramp D to Snug Harbor Road, which takes about 15 minutes.
BY CAR: Take Verazzano-Narrows Bridge to Staten Island.
Turn off onto Clove Road/Richmond Road Exit. Stay on Clove Road to Bard Road. Turn Right on Bard and follow signs to Snug Harbor.

NEW YORK
OPEN CENTER

83 Spring Street, New York, NY 10012
(between Broadway and Lafayette)
Tel: (212) 219-2527
Hours: Daily, 10 a.m.–10:30 p.m.

*O*ver the past several decades, a vast store of spiritual knowledge has emerged from around the world. Lessons abound from the earliest shamans to present-day gurus. Paths from Taoism to *A Course in Miracles* are now available in a dizzying variety of modalities and interpretations.

So much knowledge, so little time. What's a seeker to do?

Getting some perspective on it all is an enlightened first step. For this, we recommend a trip to the New York Open Center. This highly-respected institution has organized and cogently outlined major areas of study, making it easier for the student to choose a focus. Their catalogue of events contains hundreds of workshops, conferences, lectures, continuing classes, and retreats devoted to the exploration of what it means to be a whole person.

> *He not busy being born is busy dying.*
> —Bob Dylan

The center itself, where most of the classes are held, has a welcoming, low-key atmosphere, and the mostly-volunteer staff is pleased to answer your questions. A small meditation room on the second floor is open to all and serves as a welcome respite from the bustle of down-town Soho.

Don't let the size of the cozy ground-floor bookstore fool you. It contains wide and well-chosen selections of books on consciousness, creativity and spirituality as well as new age music CDs, workshop tapes, and videos of renowned teachers. You'll find that often the person behind the counter is a font of information.

Whether you are searching for a path, have found one and want to deepen your practice, are yearning for the company of fellow travelers, or simply want to enjoy a stimulating lecture, give the Open Center a try.

NEW YORK
SHAMBHALA CENTER

118 West 22nd Street, 6th floor, New York, NY 10011
(between Sixth & Seventh Avenues)
Tel: (212) 675-6544

*S*hambhala is a legendary kingdom of enlightened citizens who live in an advanced society based on fearlessness and nonagression. Shambhala—the very word holds a promise of something rich and mysterious.

The New York City Shambhala Center exudes serenity from its beautiful entryway and small rooms for teaching and private

If we open our eyes, if we open our minds, if we open our hearts, we will find that this world is a magical place.

—CHOGYAM TRUNGPA RIMPOCHE

work, to its four spacious meditation spaces. The largest is the Buddhist Meditation room, where reverence for The Venerable Chogyam Trungpa Rinpoche's lineage is expressed in loving Buddhist tradition.

The New York center, like others around the country, was founded by Trungpa Rimpoche, one of the pioneers who brought Buddhism to the West. Shambala

International is now under the guidance of his son, Sakyong Mipham Rimpoche. Its purpose is to teach the practice of meditation in both Buddhist and secular contexts.

There are so many things to do here. You can learn all levels of Trungpa Rinpoche's secular Shambhala Meditation, or simply study traditional Buddhist meditation. Classes are available in the contemplative arts such as calligraphy, Ikebana flower arrangement, tea ceremony, and Kyudo, or Japanese archery. It's definitely the place to hear talks by well-known teachers such as Pema Chodrun, the highly respected American-born Buddhist nun who is a frequent visitor.

This vibrant place welcomes visitors with many open houses and free talks on a variety of themes related to meditation and contemplation. Call to receive their schedule of events.

NEW YORK ZENDO
SHOBO JI
at THE ZEN STUDIES SOCIETY

223 East 67th Street, New York, NY 10021
Tel: (212) 861-3333

*D*efining Zen is like pointing a finger toward the moon—the finger must not be confused with the moon. That said: Zen is ancient, rigorous, spare, and disciplined. It contains no trimmings, visualizations, mantras, or feel-good messages. It is neither religion nor philosophy. It is a practice.

There are no goals, no expectations in Zen. You simply sit. This quiets the rational mind, allowing space for unencumbered awareness. Illusions about self and reality fall away. The mind returns to a place of simplicity and clarity where things can be seen as they are, not as we would like them to be.

This sounds simpler than the practice proves to be. We are reminded of the young student who, after several days of

When you study Buddhism you should have a general house cleaning of your mind.

—Zen Master Shunryu Suzuki

struggling to learn Zen meditation, asked his abbot: "What is Zazen? How do I do it?" The teacher replied: "I don't know, I haven't found out yet." The abbot had been sitting for 35 years.

At the Zen Studies Society, two meditation rooms with bare white walls lined in dark wood direct your focus inward. In each room, two rows of black zafus (pillows) face one another. Altars hold statues of the Buddha surrounded by flowers and candles. A suffusion of incense, the ceremonial ringing of bells, and the rapping of wooden clappers displace the distractions of the city. Your meditation deepens when sitting among these practitioners, motionless, in profound silence.

Not a place or practice to be taken lightly, the New York Zendo offers support and community for those sincerely interested in meditation and introspective inquiry. On Thursdays at 6:45 pm, first-timers can learn the basics of sitting and walking Zazen, after which they are invited to attend the regular sitting. A full calendar of events, and there are many, is available.

New York Zendo Shobo Ji is also associated with the Dai Bosatsu Zendo, three hours out of Manhattan in the Catskills, where retreats are offered amid 1400 acres of wilderness preserve. For information, call: (845) 439-4566.

NICHOLAS ROERICH
MUSEUM

319 West 107th St., New York, NY 10025
(between Broadway and Riverside Drive)
Tel: (212) 864-7752
Hours: Tues–Sun, 2–5 p.m. Admission: By donation.

reat art uplifts the human spirit, and a particularly wonderful experience of this kind awaits you at the Nicholas Roerich Museum. Set in a blissful three-story townhouse, more than 100 of the 7,000 paintings by this Russian master are on display to feast your eyes and nourish your soul.

Roerich believed that art could unify all of humanity and he set about to prove it through his work. His interests were widespread, but what we resonate with most are his lengthy travels high into the Himalayas where he

Art, used collectively for painting, sculpture, architecture and music, is the mediatress between and reconciler of nature and man.

— SAMUEL TAYLOR COLERIDGE

endured incredible hardships, conducting grueling horseback expeditions through Asia, Mongolia, and Turkisan in fierce cold at altitudes often as high as 15,000 feet. He was even imprisoned several times. An intense spiritual yearning propelled this man to these extremes.

Roerich's transcendent painting demonstrates his passion for the East, his search to discover man's mythic and religious roots, as well as his own personal inner truths. Because of its mysterious quality, his works cannot be squeezed into any class or school of art. Each painting is original and arresting in its mystical power. Though you can see them all in one visit, it takes several pilgrimages to give each its contemplative due.

We are continually spellbound by three works in particular: the two monks greeting one another in a snowy salmon-and-mauve half-light in "And We Do Not Fear;" the enigmatic veil covering the Mother's eyes in "Mother of the World;" and the figure of "Saint Panteleimon The Healer," hunched with age, crossing a treeless landscape, a palate of wildflowers beneath his feet.

New York artist Alex Grey says: "Mystic art establishes a visual covenant with receptive viewers, validating the boundless state and opening a portal back to spirit." These paintings linger in the heart long after leaving the museum, and no doubt you'll have the urge to tell your spiritually-minded friends about them.

The museum, which has a small but surprisingly complete shop for cards and prints, also acts as a library and archive of artifacts relating to Roerich's extraordinarily multifaceted life.

OMEGA INSTITUTE

260 Lake Drive, Rhinebeck, NY 12572-3212

Tel: (800) 944-1001

Open June through September.

*O*mega is a vibrant village in the midst of nature's bounty. There's always something going on—you can choose to be as social and active as you like, or to get away from it all to the peaceful spots on campus for rest and contemplation."

These words are from Omega Institute's catalogue. Set in the Hudson River Valley about two hours north of New York City, the campus covers 80 acres of rolling hills and woodlands with a beautiful, private lake.

Since it was founded 21 years ago, Omega has become the largest alternative education and retreat center in the country. You can choose courses from such luminaries as

Wisdom is one of the few things in human life that does not diminish with age.

—RAM DASS, *STILL HERE*

Deepak Chopra, Thich Nhat Hanh, Neale Donald Walsch, Pema Chodron, Stephen Levine, and Julia Cameron. Each season there are more than 250 workshops that stretch your mind, heal your body, open your heart, and nourish your soul. If you have little ones and would like to bring them along, not to worry: A program of activities for children 4-12 will keep them happily occupied.

The center is renowned for its community atmosphere—a great place to meet like-minded people. During a typical weekend or five-day session, there are about 300 guests on campus. In the winter months the accommodating staff numbers around 30, but that number swells to more than 200 in the spring, summer, and fall.

Omega Institute's generous brochure will answer all your questions about programs, registration, lodging, meals, prices, and travel by bus, train, or car. It's not a matter of whether you will find something to help you on your path but, rather, what to choose from the wealth of possibilities offered.

TRAVEL DIRECTIONS:

BY BUS: The Arrow charter bus leaves from the northeast corner of 31st St. and Eighth Avenue Friday and Sunday only at 4:15 p.m. Bus returns from Omega to 31st St. and Eighth Avenue Friday and Sunday only at 1:15 p.m. Fare is $25 each way. It's a three-hour ride.

BY CAR: The trip takes about 2 hours. Get Omega's brochure for its detailed directions.

PACEM IN TERRIS

96 Covered Bridge Road, Warwick, NY 10990

Tel: (845) 986-4329.

Call for hours. This home is open to the public.

*S*cientist, writer, sculptor, painter, master drawer, and practitioner of "life that knows it is living," Frederick Franck left the art world of New York City in the sixties and moved with his wife, Claske, to an old house in Warwick, New York. Over the years, he has transformed it into a work of art, a personal statement that he calls Pacem In Terris (Peace on Earth), which he dedicates to Pope John XXIII, Albert Schweitzer, and Daisetz T. Susuki—the three people Franck reveres most.

Pacem In Terris is a unique, living monument, open to the public free of charge. It contains several un-manicured sculpture gardens that serve as backdrops for Franck's massive sculptures of steel or wood with titles like "The Tree of Life," "Phoenix Rising," "Death and Transfiguration,"

> *There is no split between a man's being, his art, and what one might call his 'religion'… These three are inextricably interwoven: They are one.*
>
> —FREDERICK FRANCK

"Cosmic Fish," "Seven Generations," and "Hiroshima." Setting such profound subjects within the soft quietness of Nature tempers their power and restores a kind of wholeness to things.

In addition to the gardens, the Franck's home and Little Gallery display many of his paintings and drawings. Across the river that runs through the property is an ancient mill that has been converted into a sacred space for classical music concerts and other events.

Pacem In Terris embodies the themes of the human condition that run through Franck's life and art: creation, alienation, restoration, death, transfiguration—giant themes that work toward finding unity in human diversity. It is also an oasis of tranquility where you can find a truly deep peace.

DRIVING DIRECTIONS: Take the New York Thruway to Route 17North, to Route 17A, to Route 94. Turn left on Route 94, then turn right onto Fancher Road to the end and Pacem In Terris.

RELIGIOUS SOCIETY OF FRIENDS

15 Rutherford Place (between Second and Third Avenues)
Tel: (212) 673-5750.
Services: Sunday at 9:30 and 11 a.m.

How do you describe a Quaker Meeting where there is no minister or layperson in charge, no set form of worship, no singing, no scripture reading, in fact, no talking at all, unless the spirit moves a Friend to stand and speak her or his mind? It's just you and others, sitting silently together in a simple space, reflecting and meditating.

The small pamphlet given to visitors describes it this way: "With up to an hour of silence, we have only our own discipline to fall on: the quiet may seem hard to bear, but with others worshipping there we can feel the love and power in us all, God within and amongst us teaching us to be wide awake to what fosters good and diminishes evil, and then do something about it."

The power of this silence is unmistakable. And when

What lies behind us and what lies before us are tiny matters compared to what lies within us.

—RALPH WLADO EMERSON

someone chooses to speak, it comes from a deeply considered place which becomes meaningful to everyone. For us, this form of worship addresses one of the eternal paradoxes of what it is to be human: The need to be free, to be separate, to think your own thoughts, coupled with the equally strong need to be a part of community, to share, to be one with a group.

While inner reflection marks the center of the Quaker religion, these people also get out and "do something about" the inequities of the world. These people are activists who care passionately about peace and equality. They care for the sick and homeless with a shelter in their church. They make their voices heard about brutality of all sorts. In short, Quakers walk their talk.

There are meeting places in Brooklyn, Flushing, the Upper West Side, and Staten Island. We especially love the Meeting House downtown on Rutherford Place because of its history (built in 1860) and because it embodies the notion of Quaker simplicity. The meeting room is washed in soft grey with benches facing one another, providing no focal point, no place to rest your attention except within yourself.

RIVERSIDE CHURCH

490 Riverside Drive at 120th St.
New York, NY 10027-5788
Tel: (212) 870-6700
Sunday Service: 10:45 a.m.

*S*everal large churches in New York stretch far beyond their local communities, and Riverside Church is one of them. We first became familiar with its ministry back in the late seventies when William Sloan Coffin, Jr., then senior minister, exhorted us to rethink our attitudes about racism, equality, and peace. Through the years we have known it's ministry as broadly inclusive. All races, classes, religions (it is interdenominational), cultures, ethnicities, genders, ages, and sexual orientations are welcome and, indeed, celebrated.

Today, James A. Forbes, Jr. stands at the helm, and is every bit as charismatic and inspirational as Rev. Coffin. In a recent sermon, he reminded us that being Christian often

We are made to reach out to the transcendent. Made for the infinite.

—Archbishop Desmond Tutu

requires more of us than we are willing to give. If we were comfortable in our pews, he told us, he wasn't doing his job well enough! This is a place where spirituality is more than just Sunday talk.

The programs offered are legion and speak to many far-reaching concerns, with teams and task forces on housing, AIDS, education, peace and disarmament, prison ministry, a South African initiative, racial justice, and gay and lesbian issues. Len volunteers there, conducting conversation groups in their acclaimed English-as-a-second-language program. There are multiple Bible study and prayer groups, an active wellness center, many musical events, and much more.

The church, with its deep Nave and high Gothic arches, is modeled after Chartres Cathedral. Vibrant stained glass windows line the sanctuary and reach through the lattice of stonework behind the altar. Riverside is known for the 74-bell carillon that rings its message out over the Upper West Side.

Amazing, isn't it, that this giant 2400-member church is but one of more than 800 parishes in Manhattan alone? It's enough to assure us that the spirit is alive and well in New York City.

RIVERSIDE PARK

Entrance at Riverside Drive and 96th Street, New York, NY

*A*fter a bleak city winter, even the hardest of hearts opens on the first real day of spring. Westsiders step tentatively out of their buildings like snails from under logs and turn their pasty faces to the sun. As they head West, their pace quickens toward Riverside Park.

Choose a Saturday or Sunday around the middle of April, and enter the park at 96th Street to breathe in the ambrosia wafting from a brilliant stand of cherry trees just bursting into gaudy pinks and dancing in the breeze. You will want to applaud in appreciation. Walk past the neighborhood gardens that sing out in riotous color. See animals trot, people jog, tots wrapping their tiny fists around impossibly green grass. Experience everyone smiling in a moment of shy, miraculous joy.

Loveliest of trees
the cherry now
Is hung with bloom
along the bough,
And stands about
the woodland ride
Wearing white
for Eastertide.

— A.E. Houseman

Stop by the dog run where New Yorkers frolic with their canine companions. There's a great deal more going on here than the simple owner/pet thing. These beings are family who, if they're treated anything like our cat Tulip, often fare better than their owners. How we need our animals in this city!

Halfway along the promenade, follow the sloping path down the hill, through the tunnel and out onto the esplanade beside the splendid Hudson River. Walk as far as the 79th Street Boat Basin and check out the boats with their halyards clinking in the stiff breeze that whips up the river.

Riverside Park has its way of renewing us just like this the whole year 'round. Who knows, maybe such transcendent moments are actually made possible by the city-dweller's habit of hibernating in layers of concrete.

ROCKEFELLER STATE PARK PRESERVE AND UNION CHURCH OF POCANTICO HILLS

Pocantico Hills, NY Tel: (914) 631-1470
Hours: 8 a.m. to sunset, all year.
Call for hours: (914) 631-2069

*R*esearching this book has not only deepened our appreciation of places we've known, it has also led us to several wonderful new discoveries. We thought we were up to speed on all the natural sanctuaries a short drive from Manhattan. Then a friend told us about Rockefeller State Park Preserve.

We arrived at this nature lover's paradise on a sunny October afternoon. This natural habitat occupies 860 acres of Hudson Valley, including a 24-acre lake and an abundance of wildlife. From the 21 trails—with names like Ash Tree Loop, Peaceful Path, Witch's Spring Trail, Deer Run, and Nature's Way—we chose to walk along the 1.3 mile Swan Lake Trail. The lake was swarming with ducks and Canadian Geese, while one lone blue Heron sat watch on a branch jutting out of the water.

This landscape of shadowed voices, these
feathered bodies and antlers and tumbling
streams — these breathing shapes are our family,
the beings with whom we are engaged, with
whom we struggle and suffer and celebrate.

—DAVID ABRAM
THE SPELL OF THE SENSUOUS

The Rockefeller family designed these lush trails to take advantage of the surrounding landscape, and rode along them in horse-drawn carriages. Today you can stroll, jog, bird-watch, horseback ride, or cross country ski on them. And there are countless places to sit and connect with the wisdom of nature. Rockefeller State Park Preserve is now publicly owned. It belongs to you, so go enjoy your own piece of nature.

On your return from the preserve, be sure to stop at the Union Church of Pocantico Hills. Built in 1921, this non-denominational country church provides a unique setting for works by two modern masters, Marc Chagall and Henri Matisse. Chagall's series of nine windows depicting scenes from the Bible are the only ones he designed for a church in the United States. Matisse created the rose window above the chancel, memorializing Abby Aldrich Rockefeller. What better day than one that combines high nature with great art.

DRIVING DIRCTIONS: Take the New York State Thruway to the last Exit before the Tappan Zee Bridge. Take to Route 9 North through Tarrytown to Route 117, which takes you to the Preserve. For the Church of Pocantico Hills, take a right out of preserve onto Route 117. Turn Right onto Route 448 and go about 2 miles to the church.

ROSE MAIN
READING ROOM
at THE NEW YORK PUBLIC LIBRARY

Fifth Avenue and 42nd Street, New York, NY 10018

Tel: (212) 340-0849

*Hours: Mon 10 a.m.–6 p.m.; Tues.–Wed. 11a.m.–7:30 p.m.;
Thurs–Sat 10 a.m.–6 p.m.*

*Y*our train doesn't leave Grand Central for another hour. You're frazzled and would love some place to sit, unwind, and get back in touch with yourself.

Just cross 42nd Street to the New York Public Library. That's right, the library. Even as you walk between the lions and enter its portals, the blast of city energy immediately diminishes. Go down the long hall to the right and take the elevator to the third floor. The library's intuitive founder, John Shaw Billings, allowed in ample sunlight while preserving the quiet

> *My library was*
> *dukedom large enough.*
>
> —WILLIAM SHAKESPEARE
> *THE TEMPEST*

which would liberate readers from the bustle of the city and ennoble them and their research.

Stroll past the changing art exhibits in the long halls,

102

then take a moment to look at the magnificent murals and ornate ceilings in the McGraw Rotunda and Bill Blass Catalogue Room (315). They look like Tiepolos or Tintorettos and give an indication of what you'll see as you walk through the beautiful arched doorway leading into the splendid Rose Main Reading Room—our spot of spots for a calm space in the middle of Manhattan.

In truth, this is a library and to the left sit row upon row of people hard at work on computers. But off to the right, and well separated by a book-delivery area, you'll find the vast hush of old-time libraries, with heavy wooden tables, high windows, and books, books, books. It's the perfect place to take a breath, catch up on your journal, or close your eyes and meditate. You could even read a book.

This sprawling space stretches almost two city blocks in length and claims the distinction of being one of the largest rooms without columns in the world. The outrageous ceiling spans from end to end with gilt cherubs, grinning satyrs, and a giant mural of puffy pink and white clouds that let you pretend you are looking through to the sky. Just don't miss your train.

SAINT LUKE'S GARDEN

487 Hudson Street, New York, NY 10014
(between Grove and Barrow Streets)
Hours: Open dawn to dusk. Closed Mondays.
Note: No pets or strollers, please.

*B*arrow Street begins across Seventh Avenue from Sheridan Square and a century back in time. The human-sized calm of this narrow, crooked lane reminds us of what the city must have been like when buildings were just two or three stories high, and life had to be more simple.

As you enter through the gate to St. Luke's School, you wend your way past the church and the backs of buildings. When you see a high, glassed-in porch with wrought iron steps down to the ground, you know you're in a place time has left alone. This maze must have evolved around the church through many years and many hands.

> *Even the smallest of garden plots reveals the awesome and intricate plan behind all creation.*
>
> —Peg Streep,
> Spiritual Gardening

Down box-lined walks, past townhouse backyards, you finally arrive at St. Luke's Garden. Though it is open to the public, it feels like someone's private space. In the center, a large crabapple tree shades the walkways. Weathered benches ask to be sat upon. As you listen to happy chirping birds, let your eyes wander over stands of black-eyed susans and bee balm, and drink in the smell of honeysuckle.

While traffic thrums on the other side of the overgrown brick wall, here in the garden you'll be left to your own thoughts.

SAINT PATRICK'S CATHEDRAL

Fifth Avenue, New York, NY 10022
(between 50th And 51st Streets)
Tel: (212) 753-2261
Masses: Daily and Sunday. Call for hours.

*S*aint Patrick's intricate Gothic spires rise 330 feet above the very center of the city at Fifth Avenue and 50th Street and its leader is the Archbishop of New York. You feel the power of the cathedral immediately upon entering through huge doors that open onto the giant nave of the church.

Saint Patrick's is accustomed to constant use. People pour through it daily, some to pray, some as tourists just to see the place. Its 2,400 seats are filled to capacity regularly, and several times on Sunday. Television monitors are affixed to every pillar so that the

All things work together for good to them that love God.

— ROMANS 8:28

speaker can be seen and heard from its far reaches. Masses flow like clockwork here, as they must in order to accommodate the crowds.

Yet St. Patrick's remains a place of consummate beau-

106

ty. Light streams through intricate stained glass windows. Gothic arches soar overhead. Small altars and shrines surround the main sanctuary, each more stunning than the previous one.

So what makes this place inherently spiritual? First of all, it sits in the middle of our vast metropolis and serves it extremely well. You can come here to catch your breath at any time during the day. Appropriate or not, we've even seen people in the pews working on their computers.

Even so, it also remains a place where you can go deeply within yourself. The best spot, according to a friend who was married in Saint Patrick's, is the Lady Chapel. Its location directly behind the main altar and apart from the mainstream allows the chapel to retain a special hush and a deep sense of reverence.

SAINT THOMAS CHURCH
FIFTH AVENUE

1 West 53rd Street, New York, NY 10019

Tel: (212) 757-7013

Sweet sounds, oh, beautiful music, do not cease!

Reject me not into the world again.

With you alone is excellence and peace,

Mankind made plausible, his purpose plain.

—Edna St Vincent Millay

ore than 800 churches and nearly 100 synagogues grace the Island of Manhattan alone. To praise one as more worthy than another would be fruitless and untrue. All are sanctuaries and sacred spaces. If there were room enough to put each of these houses of worship in our book, all would be here. But alas our tome is finite, so we have chosen a few churches to represent the many, a reminder that these sanctuaries abound in our fair city, most of them awaiting visitors with open arms.

Because of their locations or other qualities, some

churches must be particularly well-equipped for the many visitors that stream in everyday, all day long. One such church is St. Thomas, situated at the busy corner of Fifth Avenue and 53rd Street.

A great reredos rises 80 feet above the altar in the main sanctuary of St. Thomas, its stone lattice of Biblical figures carved so intricately, so delicately, that the blue stained glass window behind peeps through it like light through lace.

St. Thomas has one of the finest boys' choir schools in the country, and it is put to spectacular use in the Gothic reaches of this beautiful church. In the procession you stretch to separate the high, reedy voices of the cherubic young boys from the deep tones of the men's choir that follows. From the choir stalls, their ethereal voices blend and weave through the church's towering Gothic arches as though filtering down from heaven itself.

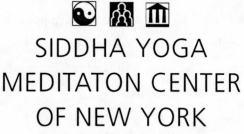

SIDDHA YOGA
MEDITATON CENTER
OF NEW YORK

230 West 29th St., New York, NY
(between Seventh and Eighth Avenues)
Satsang: Tues and Thurs at 7 p.m.
Admission: Free. Food: Inexpensive.

SYDA FOUNDATION

324 West 86th Street, New York, NY 10024
(between West End and Riverside Drive)
Tel: (212) 873-8030
Call for ashram program information.

*D*o you remember when you began wondering what life was really about? We were surprised how young some of our friends were when they realized that they were "on the path." Some recall a certain minister or Rabbi who skipped comfortable homilies and inspired them with "the deep stuff." The book *Be Here Now* seems to have turned many of us on, as did Ram Dass and Timothy Leary themselves. For others, it was that first Yoga class taught by a teacher further along the path.

The root of meditation is the Guru's form
The root of worship is the Guru's feet
The root of mantra is the Guru's word
The root of liberation is the Guru's grace.

— GURU GITA

Often the second or third step invovled stumbling upon a real-life Swami for the first time—like that mesmerizing trip to South Fallsburg, New York to see Swami Muktananda, head of the revered Siddha Yoga lineage. There are many Yoga traditions. We are told that Siddha is best characterized as a Yoga of spiritual energy combined with the grace of the Guru.

Over the years, we have visited the Siddha Ashram on West 86th St. where enthusiastic followers sang out chants, spoke of their beliefs, and meditated together, all in heavenly rooms with carpeted floors, flickering candles and worshipful pictures of the Siddha lineage. We remember when Baba Muktananda chose Gurumayi to succeed him as head of the Siddha Community. Gurumayi is a beautiful, media-savvy woman with huge liquid eyes and a radiant smile. She's also given to wearing vibrant red — not someone you forget easily once you've laid eyes on her. The community has thrived under her tutelage.

We are not surprised that the organization has out-grown the Ashram and now holds their Satsangs (open meetings where one contemplates one's experiences on the spiritual path) at a much larger temporary space on West 29th. They have thought of everything to make you feel comfortable, and the place runs without a hitch. Young devotees greet you at the door, give you a name tag, and send you downstairs. Here you remove your shoes and are welcomed to sample wonderful home-made snacks and deserts after Satsang. There is also a bookstore with tapes and books and information about other Siddha programs.

Satsang with these joyous folk is a rousing affair. A group playing authentic Indian instruments leads chant-ing as you find your seat on pillow or chair. Over a hun-dred people fill the large, spare room covered with oriental carpets. Short talks take place reverently below a stage decorated with pictures of the gurus. More chant-ing follows, then a good-length meditation ends the evening.

This is a very friendly place with lots of young people and many worthwhile programs. So is their National Headquarters at the Shree Muktananda Ashram in South Fallsburg, once called the "St. Tropez of ashrams" by the New York Post. Try a Satsang on Tuesday or Thursday night and see if it's for you.

SRI CHINMOY COMMUNITY

8600 block of Parsons Boulevard, Jamaica, New York

Tel: (718) 297-6456 or (212) 479-7878

It's rare to encounter an authentic Indian guru, unless you travel to India or some other far-away place. But one major exception lives right here in Queens.

Spiritual master Sri Chinmoy has made New York his home since the late sixties. Some of his American devotees, who number about 250, have been with him for as long as 30 years. With over 4,000 followers worldwide, the guru often travels abroad, but he calls the Queens community his home.

This thriving and varied community includes several restaurants, natural food stores, a stationary store, a barber shop, a bakery, and a clothing store—all painted

> *Smile, smile as powerfully as possible to relieve yourself of your mental tension.*
>
> — SRI CHINMOY

baby blue and bearing names such as "Smile of the Beyond Vegetarian Restaurant," "The Garden of Divinity's Love" (flower shop), "Guru Stationary," and "The

Oneness-Fountain-Heart Restaurant." Everywhere the guru's music plays softly in the background, and often a video runs, showing him praying or painting or playing a musical instrument. The restaurants post sayings by the guru on each table. One reads: "Determination can bravely and forcefully change the deplorable past into real dust." Each store and restaurant reserves a chair or some more elaborate space of honor for the guru.

Sri Chinmoy is a man of many talents. He has written over a thousand books and appears to create poetry and music continuously. Recently, we were at the dedication of a new natural food store where he improvised a chant specifically for the occasion.

The community shares a real passion for physical fitness. Sri Chinmoy, now in his late 60s, looks almost boyish, especially in his jogging attire. We understand he plays a good tennis game, and we've even seen a picture of him lifting a 7,063-pound weight—with one hand—to "demonstrate the power of inner strength." The community runs a series of races, some thousands of miles long over extended periods of time—numbers difficult for most of us to grok, though many devotees have successfully run the New York City Marathon.

Surprisingly, the group is actually quite decentralized, so much so that it has been labeled "the ashram without walls." They are all engaged in their own pursuits, and there is no specific meeting or meditation place. But they choose to live near one another, saying: "We are all on the same path, sharing the same spiritual energy. We need each other."

If you would like to see a working devotional community in action, visit the Sri Chinmoy Center. You are most welcome at all of their places of business, and the guru holds open meditations at least once a month (call for time and place). They hold concerts two to three times a year, and we are told that they will be opening a meditation center in Manhattan's East Village.

TRAVEL DIRECTIONS:
BY SUBWAY: Take the Sixth Avenue Local, F train, to Parsons Boulevard. About 30 minutes from last stop in Manhattan.
BY CAR: Take the Midtown Tunnel to the Long Island Expressway, to the Grand Central Parkway East, to Parsons Blvd. Then make a right onto Parsons Blvd. Follow to the 8600 block. Stores will be on the right. (Stationery store is #86-24)

STRAWBERRY FIELDS

Entrance: Central Park West and 72ndStreet

Admission: Free.

For his Mass for the Twenty-First Century, New York composer Carman Moore turned to Central Park for inspiration because he considers it the spiritual center of New York. Why? First, because the park acts selflessly as the lungs of the city, constantly pumping oxygen into its airless corridors. And with the skyscrapers well in the distance, the park is the one place where we can raise our eyes straight up to a full sky, a rare sight elsewhere in

> *And in the end, the*
> *love you take*
> *Is equal to the love you*
> *make.*
>
> — THE BEATLES, "THE END"
> FROM *ABBEY ROAD*

the city. Finally, this priceless piece of real estate serves as our nearest teacher of the Tao: "No squirrel ever had to worry that acorns were going to be there each fall for his winter food."

It is fitting, then, that Strawberry Fields is in Central Park. When John Lennon was assassinated nearby, the world went into mourning because his songs reflected the best in us. This garden was created by Yoko Ono in his memory. Standing across from it, a visitor is immediately touched by the unmistakable care taken with its landscape. Benches rest under shady trees, many with brass plaques commemorating loved ones. You can feel the common reverence shared by those who lie on in its lush green lawns or stroll its paths.

At the heart of this small sanctuary is a circular mosaic set into the walkway. On any given day, you will find mementos placed around it. One day in June, for instance, a candle with two white lilies decorated a picture of Robert F. Kennedy. The inscription read "Imagine No Assassins." There were also pictures celebrating Paul McCartney's birthday, and reminders of a photography exhibit of his late wife's work. This small, perfect garden has been here since 1985 and people still remember.

Strawberry Fields has been dedicated as a Garden of Peace by many nations, including Afghanistan, Israel, India, and Pakistan. Imagine peace in all those places.

SUFI MOSQUE
MASJID AL FARAH
and SUFI BOOKS

227 West Broadway New York, NY 10013

Tel: (212) 334-5212

Mon–Sat 11 a.m.–8 p.m. Closed Sundays.

*G*o to a Zikr any Thursday night at eight o'clock at the Sufi Temple Masjid al Farah. During this ritual of Divine remembrance, you will pray, you will chant, you will listen. You can ask questions of the presiding Sheik or Sheika who will answer you with wisdom and compassion. You sing. You dance. You laugh. You eat. You commune. Whether or not you plan to become a Dervish (this is not the whirling kind, but during the Zikr they do whirl) you will be inspired, entranced, and filled with the divine spirit emanating from these ecstatic people.

> *Let yourself be silently drawn*
> *By the stronger pull*
> *Of what you really love.*
>
> —RUMI

We first became interested in Sufism through the writings of author and teacher Lex Hixon, or Nur-al-Jerrahi. He was a student of all the major religions, understanding that they have an ultimate unity in the one ocean of Divine Reality. He encouraged others to do the same: "Meet as many adepts from various paths as you can. Love these persons, receive their initiations, and passionately practice their disciplines. But enter your own inner chamber of primordial awareness to enjoy selfless peace and delight."

The Sufis are the mystics of Islam. Their work is to seek knowledge; not worldly knowledge, but divine knowledge. You know the difference because mystic knowledge soothes your heart, while worldly knowledge makes you anxious. You cannot have knowledge without love, and that's what you receive from Sufis—boundless love.

Sufi Books, the store, embodies all these principals. It serves as a meeting place for Sufis and is filled with books about all the major religions, healing and spirituality, and more.

So let yourself go. Prepare to stay and have a profound and rousing time. All are welcome. *Al hum du li la!*

TEMPLE EMANU-EL

1 East 65th Street, New York, NY

Tel: (212) 744-1400

Hours: Daily, 10:00 a.m.–5:00 p.m. for meditation and prayer

Sunset service: Sun–Thurs, 5:30 p.m.
Sabbath service: Fri, 5:15 p.m. and Sat, 10:30 a.m.

*S*ynagogues and churches normally dedicate most of their work to their own congregations. But Temple Emanu-El's commitment to broader interfaith relationships, as well as their own congregation, make it particularly welcoming to all.

Temple Emanu-El, built in magnificent Byzantine-Romanesque style, is the largest synagogue in the world. Entering the main sanctuary, you face an enormous, unobstructed space of marble decorated with intricate gold tracery.

We like Cissy Grossman's description of the temple's architectural details in her book,

> *Holy, holy, holy is the*
> *Lord of hosts:*
> *The whole earth is full*
> *of his glory.*
>
> — Isaiah 6:3

The Temple Treasury: "The richness of colored light flowing from the stained-glass windows on three sides, the soft tonality of the acoustic tile walls, the high light from the timbered roof, the sparkling color and gold reflected off the variegated mosaic tiles around the arch combine to fill the huge volume with majesty and wonder."

Sitting in the silence of this vast, sacred space cleanses the spirit and opens our eyes to life in a larger context. In the more intimate Beth-El Chapel that adjoins the main sanctuary, we can savor our personal connection with the Divine. What a blessing to have such a place for meditation and prayer every day of the week.

TIBET HOUSE

22 West 15th Street, New York, NY 10011
(between Fifth and Sixth Avenues)
Tel: (212) 807-0563
Fees: Annual membership begins at $35.

During a recent visit to Tibet House we heard a talk given by its President, Columbia University Professor of Buddhism, Robert Thurman, who is renowned for making Buddhism accessible to Americans. His stream of insights reminded us that the essence of Buddhism is freedom from suffering, and that we can all realize this freedom through Buddhist knowledge and practices.

Ironically, the thousand-year-old Tibetan Buddhist civilization—the embodiment of genius, peace, and harmony—is today being threatened with imminent extinction. Tibet House is part of a worldwide network committed to ensur-

> *It is the enemy who can truly teach us to practice the virtues of compassion and tolerance.*
>
> —THE DALAI LAMA

ing that the light of the Tibetan spirit, which arises from wisdom and compassion, never disappears from the face of the Earth. This is a place with a mission.

Sacred mandalas hang on the walls and a vibrant shrine room with a beautifully sculpted golden Buddha calls all to meditation. In its small, comfortable library you can study all things Tibetan. An art gallery maintains ongoing exhibits like the contemporary renditions of the original 17th century Tibetan medical atlas paintings. Tibetan medicine differs so radically from our own that only now is its relevance being deciphered by Western medicine.

Tibet House offers a wealth of programs: conferences and lectures on spiritual philosophy, mind science, human development, intercultural dialogue, nonviolence, and peace. Members are invited to events where they can meet the leading figures and scholars in the fields of Tibetan history, art, and religion, as well as meditation teachers, artists, poets, and performers.

Of course, non-members are welcome to visit and attend lectures. However, if you join the organization, you not only have an opportunity to learn about Tibet's ancient art, culture and deep spirituality, you will also be supporting the great Tibetan nation in exile.

TRINITY CHURCH

74 Trinity Place, New York, NY 10006
(between Broadway and Wall Street)
Tel: (212) 602-0747

and SAINT PAUL'S CHAPEL

Broadway at Fulton Street, New York, NY
Tel: (212) 602-0800

*W*alking through the narrow tunnels of Wall Street, pressed in on all sides by huge buildings, it's a great relief to come out upon the delicate brown spires of Trinity Church and, a few blocks north, the smaller St. Paul's chapel. Each is like a tiny gem, with bright patches of green grass contrasting markedly against their giant gray neighbors.

A new commandment
I give unto you,
That ye love one another.

— JOHN 13:34

It's hard to believe that when these churches were built in the late 1700s, they towered over everything around them. Trinity, possibly the most famous of all New York's churches, was "inside the Wall" of the Dutch colony, which is how this financial district got its name. St. Paul's lies "outside," and therein lies their difference: One is large and majestic; the other, which was attended by nearby farmers and people from across the river in New Jersey, is smaller and simpler. Of course, President Washington attended both churches when New York City was capital of the United States of America.

St. Paul's Chapel has the distinction of being the oldest public building in continuous use on the Island of Manhattan. It was built in 1766, which pre-dates even the Declaration of Independence. Its age and simplicity, reminiscent of a more sober, less-populated time, make us wonder how we managed to develop into such a populous, materialistic society. Yet this institution remains as much a force deep in the secular heart of our nation as it was when it was built more than 200 years ago.

WAINWRIGHT HOUSE

260 Stuyvesant Avenue, Rye, NY 10580

Tel: (914) 967-6080

*W*ainwright House has the honor of being the oldest nonprofit, nonsectarian, holistic, educational center in the United States. For nearly 50 years, seekers have visited this sacred place to explore spirit, self, connection to the global community, and the call to service.

In any give season, expect to find programs ranging from Celtic Spirituality to Zen Buddhism, from Health and Wellness to the Kabbalah, and everything in between. You'll also find gentle weekends dedicated solely to relaxation and rejuvenation.

All this takes place in a beautiful mansion resting on grounds that slope down to Long Island Sound. Inside, multiple libraries, solariums, lovely dining rooms, and private meeting rooms make it a perfect place for non-profit conferences as well as personal study.

We hammer wood for a house, but it is the inner space that makes it livable.

— Tao Te Ching

Arriving from the city, your retreat begins as soon as

you smell the fresh breezes rising from the water, gaze at manicured lawns and plantings, and hear the sound of geese flying overhead.

Guests sleep in friendly double, triple, quad, or dorm-style rooms. A separate house on the grounds has its own facilities. Prices begin at $75 per day, meals included.

TRAVEL DIRECTIONS:

BY TRAIN AND TAXI: Metro North trains leave regularly from Grand Central , a 40-minute ride. Taxis are available at the station, a five minute ride.

BY CAR: From I-95, take Exit #19 toward Playland. At the first stoplight, turn right onto Milton Road and follow to the end. At flashing light, turn left onto Stuyvesant Avenue. Wainwright House is 6/10 of a mile on the right.

ZEN PALATE

663 Ninth Avenue, New York, NY 10035
(corner of 46th Street)
Tel: (212) 582-1669.
Reservations: (212) 582-1276

A year or so ago, we met a friend for lunch at this popular West Side Restaurant. We had just placed our orders when suddenly, the normally happy, somewhat noisy ambience fell to spoon-drop silence. We looked up just as all the waiters dropped to their knees, touching their foreheads reverently to the floor. This behavior totally mystified us until a parade of six saffron-robed Tibetan monks filed out of one of the dining rooms. As they passed by, a particularly wizened elder seemed to bless us all. When the monks left the restaurant, the waiters rose and continued their duties as if nothing out of the ordinary had taken place.

Welcome to Zen Palate. Who says a place has to be somber, quiet, and without joy to qualify as sacred? This beautiful place is as full of the spirit as any we can think of in this city. Its décor of soft ochre-flocked walls, rich wood, and fresh flowers is spanking clean. In the main dining room books on Buddhism line the wall beside a small statue of the Buddha adorned with candles and flowers. You can dine on vegetarian delicacies with names like "Jewel of Happiness," "Wheel of Dharma," "Zen Retreat," and "Tapestry Embrace." Steaming dishes fly out of the kitchen piled on plates like so many eccentric sculptures.

Zen Palate: A perfect example of how a happening place rooted in the hum and success of New York City can also revel in its connection to a higher power. It's certainly one of our favorite respites.

There are two other Zen Palates in the city, each with its own character. One is at 34 Union Square (212-614-9291); the other is at 2170 Broadway, between 76th and 77th Streets (212-501-7768).

ACKNOWLEDGEMENTS

WHENEVER WE BROUGHT UP THE SUBJECT OF this book, our friends were eager to share their favorite places with us. We are particularly grateful to some who have continually inspired us along the way: Edith Alston, Bob Cunniff, Kira Ferrand, Jane Gignoux, Joel and Trudy Goldsmith, Alex and Alysson Grey, Heidi Gutman, Judith Handelsman, Gail Horton, Jerry Jones, Richard Kalin, Nancy Kanter, Victoria Kaufman, Margaret Lloyd, Leonard Marks, Carman Moore, Ted May, Bruce Sherman, Lisa Simon, Alice Slater, Toby Tarnow, Rick Testa, and Lynn Yeakel.

We are especially grateful to Barbara Legowski who was so generous with her time and editorial comments; to Pat and Keith Mielke whose house, now ours, has been a haven during the final stages of preparation; and finally, to our good friend Sandra Martin whose idea it was to write this book and whose steadfast support made completing it possible.

INDEX BY CATEGORY

COMMUNITIES

DAY TRIPS

GARDENS

LIBRARIES AND BOOKSTORES

MUSEUMS

NATURE WALKS

OVERNIGHTS

House of The Redeemer / 60

Mohonk Mountain House / 72

Omega Institute / 88

Wainwright House / 128

RESTAURANTS

Ayurveda Café / 14

Hangawi Korean Restaurant / 52

Zen Palate / 130

SUFI

Sufi Mosque Masjid Al Farah and Sufi Books / 120

Printed in the United States
92747LV00004B/3/A